Lessons From Littleton

LEVELLING

A Guide To Positive Parenting

LESSONS FROM LITTLETON

LEVELLING

A GUIDE TO POSITIVE PARENTING

Dr. Brian Brody and Sandy Petersen

ISBN 0-9618074-9-0

PRINTED IN THE UNITED STATES OF AMERICA

For questions or if you need help with your Levelling Program, please call or write to:

Institute For Integration Therapy (I.F.I.T.)
P.O. Box 620430
Littleton, Colorado 80162
(303) 979-0319
www.AscendCoaching.com
e-mail: DrBrody@AscendCoaching.com

Levelling may be used as a fund-raiser for a charity or non-profit organizations. Call or write to the number listed above for more information about how Levelling can help.

We invite your comments and suggestions...

IN MEMORY OF THOSE WHO
PERISHED AT COLUMBINE HIGH SCHOOL

Contents

Acknowledgments

I thank Pam, my wife, for her love, support and devotion. I thank her for helping develop this book with me.

I thank my two, adopted children, Liz and Pete, for their love, with choice, and not because they had to.

The challenge of being a parent has taught me how much my parents truly loved me. I thank my parents who valued their children and family so much that I have a place in my heart that always feels love and acceptance. I thank my sister for being the sweetheart she is and loving me no matter what. I thank my brother for growing up to be the man that I can truly talk with.

I thank my friend Marc for his years of support, counsel and faith. I thank my friend Mary for always being there and believing in the dignity of my spirit.

I thank Cheryl Friederich and Jean McGeary for their devoted work in supporting my vision for helping children and families. Thanks for keeping the office running!

I thank Judy and Rich Broyles for their brilliance as parents and the ideas they shared in the section of the "separating adolescent".

I thank the many parents and families that I have worked with and learned so much from. Parenting is truly one of the hardest and most rewarding jobs there is. Owner's manual not included! Thank you all for the "earned miracles" I have had the honor to share with you.

I thank Joyce Hansen for her office support and ideas in which to develop this book.

I thank Susan Stewart for her editing and book design.

I thank Gary Petit at Starwest Productions for his marketing and technical support in the development of "Levelling".

I thank the staff, kids and families of the Adams County District #12 Schools for the original concept of "Levelling" that we used in the self-contained, special education classrooms.

Preface

I love my community in Columbine - Littleton, Colorado. I moved here 14 years ago to work, live and raise my children. I picked this place because it is beautiful, has nice homes and is a down to earth suburb with grounded family values.

In the late 1980's I began to see a pattern develop with many teenagers in all areas of the country. There was a dramatic increase of destructive behavior that resulted in suicides in epidemic proportion. Another phenomenon occurred. Small groups of "at risk" kids banding together to form a type of family replacement for each other. They were very structured groups telling their members how to dress, what music to listen to, what to think and what was acceptable behavior. Some of the groups were devoted to certain negative values such as suicide, death and cutting themselves. One such group was called "Death walkers". They wore black clothes, make-up and listened to music with death as the message. This was a form of what I called "Kiddie Cults". A "Cult" means a group that is devoted to a certain type of worship. Hate, anger and violence was becoming part of the devotion.

Since then we have seen more and more violence from the teen culture. Recently, the tragic rampage and massacre in Littleton. My heart is broken. I am emotionally in shock, terror and grief with so many others. Intellectually and professionally I was not surprised. It is a manifestation of an isolated and violent "kiddie cult" (suburban gang) that called themselves the "trenchcoat mafia". What scares us all is the deeper knowledge that Littleton was not an isolated incident. That it can happen in any community.

I have found that many kids in the suburbs are overindulged and simply lack the structure they need to be in better control of their lives. Without the proper structure and guidance, children do not learn the coping skills they need to adapt. Loving parents who mean well easily fall into the "rescuing trap". They "run interference" for their children. We want to give our children more than we got. We hurt when our children hurt. We want to fix it for them. We don't expect them to do a better job fixing it for themselves.

Children need to be listened to and helped to learn the problem solving skills necessary for healing. They also need the limits to halt negative patterns. When pain and lack of limits combine in a teen, we often see a serious result. There has always been and will always be trauma and pain in all our lives. The lack of structure and self-discipline has prevented many teenagers from being able to, at least, contain their rage.

I hope and pray that our society has now bottomed out in its learning process. It is time for all of us in society to stop condoning the forms of violence in video games, language, the music etc. It is all of our responsibility to "say no" to the violence in any form. It lies mostly with each family and parent to provide the model for a learning environment at home. Children learn through daily, positive repetitions that become habits that are internalized as values. What we value can also be a choice. So many kids "at risk" are our best and our brightest. They can learn that "positive is possible".

I newly revised this book just before the tragedy in Littleton. The urgency of our current crisis motivated me to put a cover on it and get it to print. The information in this book contains the lessons I have learned from the many children here in Littleton, including my own. This book is the result of the structure we utilized at home to save our own children's lives.

For ten years, I have been trying to sound the alarm about "kiddie cults", now violent teen cults, and the growing trend of violence. I have spoken to millions of people trying to sensitize and teach that there ARE answers to the problems our children face. There is not a suburb far enough away now for any of us to run away from the virus in our culture. We parents must face the contagion head on and TAKE OUR STAND HERE.

The following two articles were written ten years before the Columbine shooting.

The Suburban Youth Cult: 1989
A Violent Alternative to the Nuclear Family

By Dr. Brian Brody, MSW, LCSW, Psy.D. and Sandy Petersen

Suburban gangs, also known as cults or "kiddie cults" as I refer to them, have proliferated greatly in the past two years. A variation on the city gang, the "kiddie cult" infests the suburbs, where traditionally, the "best and brightest" are spawned in an environment that is able to meet much more than the child's basic needs, but also provide leadership and direction for it's children. Or so we thought.

All children rebel; emancipation from the parent takes a variety of forms. However, what is occurring in these gangs and cults is not harmless rebellion. Many of the suburban cult members express their separateness through wearing all black clothing, earrings, shaved heads or extreme (and often colorful) hairstyles that require the aid of several pounds of mousse or hair spray to maintain. Unconventional appearance, however, is not the thrust of my observations. All individuals identify themselves with some group. All individuals have a need to belong, to be a part of some family. The identification that is occurring with today's teens goes much deeper than surface appearance. The children in gangs, groups, and cults are in search of a surrogate family, a family that provides them with the structure, limits and discipline that is lethally lacking in their experience of their nuclear family.

We parents of these children were sowing our own wild oats in the 60's, a decade that promulgated a philosophical break-through to staid norms. Love and outright rejection of the "Establishment" was what we believed was needed to counter-act the harshness of the excessive discipline we perceived as our heritage from our parents. Love was what was needed to engender love and respect for self and others. A new genera-tion thus re-invented the art of parenting, and believed that love and "leaving well enough alone" was the answer to raising healthy, happy and productive children. It is not my intent to say that parenting as the 60's generation experienced it could not have used some qualification, but rather to point out that the parenting pendulum swung the other direction, omitting a few critical details, i.e., structure and discipline.

What the suburban kiddie cults have to offer our children is precisely what is missing in the home: the structuring of their lives. To live with structure, to live with discipline, is to understand that there are limits to behavior, that there are consequences for actions. Too many of today's youth have not had to confront the consequences of their own negative behavior. Parents have been over-protective, and over-rescuing, rushing to the aid of the errant child. The child perceives that mommy or daddy will always be there to bail him out, so he can continue behaving, as he will. This manifests as the child pushes his behavior to extremes, actually trying to force the parent to impose some limits. Additionally, the parental message is that the child is incapable of solving his own problems. The child does not develop coping skills, and cannot manage his own life.

While stylized appearances are encouraged by the cults, there is an attendant expectation that members will abide by the rules. This belonging has its price. There is little latitude of choice. One is expected to embrace the group ideology, which can mean violating the self (a phenomenon of kiddie cults), or violating others (as in city gangs), among a variety of destructive behaviors. The frustration of no limits, of no sense of selfhood, is expressed as violence, including the consideration and act of suicide or murder. As insidious is the demand that kiddie cult members will cultivate emotional depression, and sport morbid make-up and clothing. The pendulum has indeed swung again, this time from love to violence.

Death and violence are central themes for the "Death walkers" and many other cults who may also incorporate Satanic symbols as another means of rebelling against the culture that expected little or nothing of them, in the name of love.

It is alarming to note that suburban kiddie cults are spreading rapidly in this country. In some areas, they are networking-establishing home centers where a child may find refuge as a runaway. There is an emerging peculiarity with respect to these kiddie cults; historically, those children who have sought identification with gangs and cults were misfits, lacking the desire or ability to set goals for themselves. They were the academic dropouts, the punkers, the rockers, deliberately socially offensive and unresponsive to traditional counseling or therapeutic intervention.

These ranks have been joined by the "all-American" kid, the model student and leader from whom much is expected, and who is groomed to perpetuate the highest ideals of American society. College-bound "preppies" and athletic stars have formed their own cults, and in this context, are displaying a distressingly dark side. They are perpetrators of violence themselves, physically attacking members of the dropout cults. In growing numbers, these model students are covert drug abusers and are suicidal.

We must realize that the causative factor in all of these cults is lack of structure in the environment; this causes a lack of internal structure in our emerging adults. These kids are angry and hurting deeply; the formation of these cults cannot hope to resolve the problems created by lack of limits and discipline in the home. Children become fanatic devotees of their cults in an effort to find limits and self-identity, only to discover that the cults promote group identity over that of the individual's. This creates identity loss in addition to the feelings of being unable to cope in a hostile world.

The psychological climate is severely destructive, and will continue to remain so as long as parents and adults are unable to provide our children with the limits they seek. These kiddie cults have not emerged from a vacuum, and their blatant presence-an American culture in minor-is a loud cry for help.

We as parents and educators must begin to teach our children coping skills. We must step back and allow our children to make mistakes, and to learn from those mistakes. We must allow them to hurt, and not rescue them from the consequences of their own actions. Instead of telling them what to do, we must redirect authority back to them, asking what steps they can take to solve their own problems, and help them to evaluate the consequences of their behaviors. In this way, children are encouraged to develop personal coping skills-the belief in self-competence and self-esteem. Without these, our children flounder, and are the inevitable prey to whatever circumstances appear to promise a way out: running away, cults or suicide.

Troubled teens turn to cults for relief

Bill Briggs of the Denver Post wrote the following story (excerpted here) which appeared in the Denver Post on January 15, 1989:

A growing number of troubled Denver-area teenagers are turning to "kiddie cults" that promote suicide, drug abuse or Satanism, say police and mental health experts.

"What's scary is we're seeing more and more of these groups all the time," said Jefferson County psychotherapist Brian Brody. "They are there for kids to use to drop out of their lives, to run away from their families and stay on the run."

The so-called kiddie cults are highly structured groups that require members conform to strict dress codes, ideologies and musical tastes.

Death walkers, for example, dress in black, wear white makeup and listen to heavy-metal music laced with pro-suicide lyrics. Members sometimes engage in self-mutilation.

In some ways, the cults have become the suburban equivalent of urban gangs: They both draw youths who use clothing, language and violence to fuse a link among them.

There have long been school cliques-whether it was the leather-wearing greasers of the 1950's or the sport-minded jocks of the 1980's. But the cults pose serious problems for police and mental health professionals.

"The kids are getting lost in it," Brody said.

A dangerous common denominator is violence, whether it is directed inward or outward.

"They are rebelling with violence," Brody said. "They show parents they have control by hurting themselves."

Said Aurora Police Sgt. Monte Lenders: "They're all looking for something to hold onto. They need to feel they are part of something and their parents and schools aren't providing that."

The cults fill the void, say several former members.

"It's just a feeling of belonging, you need to get close to people," said 17-year-old John, befriended two years ago by a group of Death walkers.

"You need to identify with people. You need to have people you can trust," said Carol, an 18-year-old community college student who at 16 ran away from home for a summer to be with other friends in a cult.

In assuming the role of the family, kiddie cults provide members with a value system and a sense of unity many teens are searching for.

"I think that's why you don't miss your family so much," while on the run, Carol said.

Denver area school officials stress that many middle school and high school students dress in black and wear white makeup, but only a fraction of those belong to cults.

Of those that do belong, however, most eventually run away from home for weeks or months. Many also drop out of school.

Said John: "You want more control to do what you want, and you want to do it on your own. That makes your parents listen to you and see you have power too."

"There were parents who were really accepting of it and took me in," John said. "They gave me a token phrase like, "You'd better call your parents." But they weren't too concerned about it."

A parent who knowingly shelters a runaway can be charged in Colorado with contributing to the delinquency of a minor-a misdemeanor.

Running away is not a violation of the law.

"That's a status offense," Landers said. "They are not prosecuted for running away. If caught, they're taken back to their home or to a foster home."

To combat the cult problem, many parents have turned to support groups like *Tough Love*, a national organization of support groups for adults whose children are going through behavioral problems.

Said Carol: "You can sense parents when they're not kidding around and they're sick of messing with you."

Once home, the parents and their children are urged to establish ground rules under which both sides can live. That way, the teenagers get the structure they were seeking.

"Because kids are rebelling, they don't want to be told rules," Brody said. "So there's a fine line parents have to walk to present structure at home."

Introduction

Because every parent's ultimate goal is to have secure, happy, well-adjusted children and a peaceful home life, I want to share the philosophy on which the concept of Levelling is based.

Philosophically, our responsibility as parents is to teach our children values, self-esteem, self-respect, coping skills, and the ability to show love to others. We can teach these qualities by providing good examples as we parent (modeling), and by providing an environment in which our children can test their thoughts and feelings through their behavior.

Practically speaking, our job as parents and the greatest loving act we can do for our children is to raise them to be independent of us, and to function successfully in our society. Levelling helps us to do this in a sane, structured way, which allows us, as parents, to spend minimal time supervising and disciplining. In this way Levelling allows us the quality time we all want to have with our children.

Levelling will show you how you can gradually guide your children as they grow, to emerge from a primarily dependent role to independent adulthood. In this way, we spare our children the shock of finding that life outside our home is difficult or impossible to deal with. We can enjoy a loving relationship with them without guilt or resentment or feeling as though no matter what we do, we can never do enough.

Through testing and feedback, I have learned that children develop values (caring, helping, etc.) through succeeding in their endeavors without our help or interference. This is first modeled from parents and done for approval, a reward, or to avoid negative consequences. As an outgrowth of "doing" to get rewards or to please others, our children develop self-esteem and the desire to do tasks to the best of their ability to please themselves. When our children develop self-esteem and self-respect, they quite naturally are able to be helpful and loving towards others in addition to learning empathy through an understanding of the effort involved in giving.

In addition to teaching children self-respect and values, Levelling minimizes arguments and power struggles by aligning us with our children on the same side of each issue. Parents no longer need to decide every little thing every minute of the day. Through Levelling, we're no longer the unreasonable ogre in the house always telling our children what to do, what not to do and when to do it. We save time and our sanity when we have all the questions answered before they're asked, and this opens up a whole new level of loving communication.

I hope that this book will prove to be as effective and helpful to you as it has for the many families now enjoying Levelling.

Brian Brody

The Princess

Did you know that I am mother to the only princess in the world?

I've heard tell that all little girls are princesses but please don't believe that - There is Only One! She was so small and helpless with her golden red hair and she taught me to be grown and how to love.

I watched her as her body streaked from first step to adolescence and appreciated with the wondering world that there could be such beauty in human form. I saw her carrying puppies and friends, delight at the animals in the zoo, eat her first mouthful of sand - She Hated That! I held her as she cried the tears of growth and learned of this world. I smiled with pride when she gave of her resources to those in need, never considering that there should be return. Now, when I look, I see a blooming radiance that is without equal. She does not know the impact on those who pause to observe. She hasn't the experience yet to know how her openness and love shine through to those she blesses with a smile. Oh yes, you may think there are many princesses in this world, but you are wrong. There is *only one* and she is Lovely.

Mom

Son Day

There's a tow-headed boy showing off on his new skateboard. He jumps on and flows down the hill-a tower of budding masculine grace.

All pride a bluster in his newfound skills. He's 11 years old today and showing evidence of adulthood taking root. As I smile at his performance I remember all the years-his triumphs and tragedies and feel joy and gladness in his smile, easy manner, and mastery.

He is my son and I've told him, "I wouldn't trade him for a grasshopper or even a snake." I've told him how glad I am that he chose me for his mom.

You see, to me, he is the manifestation of love.

Mom

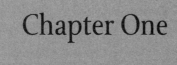

Chapter One

THE LEVEL CONCEPT

❖

A Game For Your Kids.

❖

A Game Plan For You.

Welcome to the World of Levelling

The concept of Levelling is simple. It is a structured discipline system that allows children to:

1. Know the rules so parents don't slip into the "You're grounded for the rest of your life" mistake.
2. Show responsibility before they get privileges.
3. Determine by their behavior how much freedom they can handle.
4. End the "power struggle" and badgering which makes parenting so difficult.

Levelling has been used successfully in homes with children ranging from pre-school to emancipation. It has been utilized successfully in situations where a child or children spend as little as two days per week in the Level concept (shared custody).

I suggest that you read through this Levelling book one time before you begin to set up Levelling in your home. As you do, please take the time to look at the sheets included in Chapter Nine when they're referenced in this text. Next, re-read this book and decide as you do, how you will adapt Levelling to your home. There are three "cut out" pages marked "notes" included in Chapter Nine. As you read through the first and second time, you may find it helpful to have these pages accessible for jotting down thoughts and page numbers. I have included insights, articles, poetry, and other items you may find of interest in frames interspersed throughout the text. These additions are not a part of the Levelling concept per se, but are included because I have found that they are helpful, educational, or entertaining.

I realize that there are as many girls as boys who will benefit from Levelling. However, for ease of writing, I will refer to the children as "he."

Though most parents find they don't need it, a hot line for problems and questions is available. Please feel free to either call or write at your convenience with any questions, insights or feedback you may have.

Drug Abuse and Suicide in Youth

By Brian Brody, MSW, LCSW (Excerpt from - Letters to the editor) The Denver Post

In the county where I live, there has been approximately one adolescent suicide a month for the past two years. This alarming trend is not limited to my community. Adolescent drug and alcohol usage and suicide have become a national tragedy that is assuming epidemic proportions.

In my private practice as a psychotherapist, I have observed a commonality among suicide, substance abuse and behavior problems in our children. The child who suffered through his parent's divorce, moving and losing his friends, and then a stepparent demanding that he reassume his role of child instead of caretaker in his family, hanged himself.

He was suffering from the same problems as the child who was an overachiever, captain of his baseball team and maintained a straight – A average, but who took his life after a fight with his girlfriend. Both children were also at high risk for substance abuse.

We must ask ourselves what is going on in our society; what is causing our children to seek such tragic answers to their problems?

The answer lies in two concepts: coping skills and lack of control. As parents and a society, we are overprotecting our children, thereby limiting their ability to learn how to deal with and solve their own problems.

In the first case, the child lost the structure and familiarity in his life. He compensated for these losses by taking over the caretaker role in his family. When his mother remarried, he lost the role of caretaker – the last perceived vestige of control over his life.

In the second example, an overachiever perceived that his successes were the result of people outside of himself (Mom made me study and get A's; the coach taught me everything about baseball). When his girlfriend threatened to break up with him, he believed that she knew what a fraud he really was and that he could do nothing on his own. In short, he believed he had no control over his life.

The path to suicide or substance abuse is really straightforward. The thoughts that go through a child's mind run down a predictable road from "I don't like my life; I'm hurting." The child may try to anesthetize the pain with alcohol or drugs. Since these children perceive that they have no control over their lives to change things for the better, they slip into hopelessness: "I don't like my life; I'm hurting and I can't change it." The final step is, "I can't go on this way; I can't change anything; anything is better than hurting this way; I want out." The way out, too often, is substance abuse or death.

We as parents and professionals need to help our children to learn that "failure" is really a way to learn new and better ways of dealing with things. We need to allow them to make mistakes, pay the price and learn that this isn't the end of the world, but a way to become better and stronger.

We must help our children to believe they have control and grow into assuming control of their lives, starting on the inside (knowing what they want) and moving to the outside (learning how they can get what they want, instead of depending upon us to get it for them).

Suicide and drug abuse are not only preventable, but are manifestations of the same cause. If we can allow our children to stand on their own two feet and support and counsel, rather than "running interference" for them, they will gain the ego strength necessary to succeed through trying, falling, trying again and succeeding.

No Simple Answer To Teen Suicide

By Stephen Kalat, Ph.D., (Excerpt from - Letters to the editor) The Denver Post

Brian Brody's contention that too much love sets conditions for teen suicide (Post, July 18) is one simple explanation, but too simple. Permissiveness, over-rescuing kids from problems they create, the lack of clear limits, all contribute to one part of the problem when children haven't yet learned to be responsible to others for themselves.

But equally damaging are overly punishing parental styles, where listening is minimal, and where criticism, emotional abuse or physical abuse damage self-esteem down to the core. Then there are some great conflicts in some families, where one parent is passively permissive, in part because the other parent is controlling and aggressive. Add in any alcohol abuse among parents or teens, and you have additional fuel for disaster.

The picture of teen suicide is a complicated one, with no one profile. Psychological evaluations for depression or when dangerous impulsive acts first appear, commitments to a caring, reasonable approach to discipline, and training in managing conflicts for parents and children are all potentially helpful ingredients in suicide prevention.

Reason Teenagers Choose Suicide Is Simple

By Brian Brody, MSW, LCSW (Excerpt from - Letters to the editor) The Denver Post

Dr. Stephen Kalat's response to the teen suicide issue (Letters, July 25) is perhaps as overcomplicated as he suggests my views are oversimplified. I stated, and strongly believe; that the reason our children are choosing to end their lives is simple.

To restate the quote from Bill Briggs' article (Post, July 18), "kids are dying because they don't have the coping or problem-solving skills needed to get control of their lives."

In hundreds of suicidal cases and with my two stepchildren, I have seen one process lead to the suicide attempt:

1. A problem or problems causing the individual moderate to extreme pain.
2. The concept or belief that there is nothing the individual can do to end the pain.
3. The ensuing belief that the individual will suffer this pain for the rest of his or her life.
4. The realization that there is something the individual can do — take his own life.

I became aware of this process through counseling hundreds of children and adults who desired to, or tried to, take their own lives.

The common denominator in avoiding suicidal thoughts and actions is the ability to see an end to the pain, a solution to the problem.

Parents either teach their children that they can solve their own problems, by allowing them to do so, or they fail to teach this, by solving the child's problems and conveying the message that the child is incapable of solving problems.

The Level Concept

Why Structure Your Children?

Why is structure so important to your child's emotional well being? Rules and laws give us security. Most parents change the rules according to their mood. Ruth, one of my clients, tells the story of being a single parent and daily altering the rules for her son, John. If her work day had gone well, she would let things slide by. Conversely, if the day had been tough, she was tough. John would occasionally come in at twilight (his curfew was before dark). If Ruth had a good day at work, she would ask why he was late. He would give his excuse and she would ask him to try to do better the next time. If Ruth had a stressful day, however, she would ground John for a week and two days later would forget that she had grounded him and let him go out. To one degree or another, I believe all parents are guilty of this lack of structure. After all, we're only human.

The effect of this kind of environment on our children is incredibly stressful and that is why all authorities admonish us to be consistent! Imagine how you would feel if our laws changed daily according to how a particular policeman felt. Let's say you were given a ticket for walking down the right side of the street on Monday. By Tuesday, you had learned your lesson and walked on the left side of the street. But the same policeman gives you another ticket and says, "I changed my mind, you should have walked on the right side!" Placing yourself in this situation, you are probably feeling frustrated, afraid, and as though you can't win, which is exactly what our children feel when we change the rules and punishments. Structure, rules and laws give us the opportunity to achieve—something we can't live without.

This is why, at the core of Levelling are written levels, rules and consequences. Using these written "laws" allows everyone to know what to expect. When I, as a parent, first began the Levelling concept, my children were constantly reminding me what the consequences were for what they had done: they loved and still love knowing what to expect! I love not having to stop family life every few minutes to decide what to do about every single incident or question! Be aware that when you set up your structure, you will not be able to anticipate every situation. I suggest that you add to and modify the rules as situations come up or things change. Don't be afraid to fine tune and tell your children that you are changing or adding a rule.

Structure gives us control of our lives. As we grow and mature, we test out actions and ideas, we learn what reactions we will get from other people, and what consequences to expect, thus we control our own fate. My experience with one type of child who contemplates suicide is that they perceive that they have lost control of their lives. Mom and Dad fight their battles for them and place expectations on them and set goals for them. Friends determine what they'll wear or do. Children who learn healthy coping skills have control over their own lives. With secure, loving relationships in a structured home they are much more likely to resolve their problems than to use drugs, try to deaden emotional pain, or to contemplate suicide.

Depending on how structured your home was before Levelling, you may experience your child's resistance to the new system. In cases where a home has had very little structure or a child has gotten negative attention in the past, the resistance can escalate to out-and-out rebellion. In one unusual case, this rebellion lasted 4 weeks, and nearly drove the parents to abandon the system. Don't give up hope!! The parents involved stuck with it. They now have happier, more secure children and a harmonious home life.

Please note, that to avoid "bottom line" rebellion, ("I don't care what level I'm on, I'm not going to do it") it is necessary to have the child who totally refuses to follow the system to retire immediately to his room. It is suggested that all toys, radios, books, or any other form of entertainment be removed, thus utilizing boredom to gain your child's cooperation. When banished to his room, the child should be told, "You may rejoin the family when you are ready to follow the rules."

Keep in mind that the Level System you and your children devise is not written in cement. If you find that you are feeling frustrated, there's nothing wrong with dropping the system for a time, although parents who do, find that after a few weeks their children often revert back to previous negative behavior. At this point you will probably want to reinstate the system with or without changes.

It is important to remember that, in varying degrees, your child's security and happiness depends on a structured environment. If you find yourself circumventing your own system by arguing and power struggling with your children, stop and think! Go back to the structure you have created through Levelling, and put all the rules back in force. Try reinstituting the rules with a "Coaching", more assertive style.

More or Less Work?

Levelling can, if you choose, involve charts as a memory aid for you and a means of letting your child know where he stands at all times with regard to freedoms and consequences. This causes some parents (especially the primary care giver) to believe that Levelling could make more work.

When my client, Ruth, first started adapting Levelling into her home, she felt that she'd be spending much more time monitoring, charting, and checking up on the kids than she was presently spending in power struggling with them. To her surprise, and that of other Levelling parents, the opposite was true. Levelling drastically reduced the time spent making decisions, arguing and explaining. You will be delighted to find that the time spent making decisions about whether something is acceptable or not, what punishment is appropriate, and asking your child over and over to do something, will not be necessary. Levelling will give you much more time to enjoy your children and your sanity! The writing and charting frees a parent from constantly having to repeat the, "Why nots" and the "Why can'ts" which cause parenting to be so frustrating. It aligns parents and children on the same side. Instead of endlessly explaining, you can now say, "I'd love for you to have John spend the night. Go check what level you are on." If the child is on level one and this is a level two privilege, you can say, "Darn, I'd really like for John to spend the night. Maybe by next week, you can be on level two and we'll have him over!"

In addition, once the system is allowed to function in your home, you will find a great reduction in the stress of parenting. Stress is caused in part from constantly having to evaluate a situation and react—often at a moment's notice—and from not having "standard" answers to fall back on. Of course, parenting decisions cannot be completely "by rote;". However, Levelling eliminates as many of those difficult situations (Is this behavior acceptable? What punishment is appropriate? Has his behavior been good enough to allow him to go to the movies?) as possible.

I have spoken about Coping Skills repeatedly in the Levelling text and wanted to define them for parents who may be unfamiliar with the term.

What Are Coping Skills?

Coping skills are the way we act in and react to the world. More important, coping skills are how we handle problems and adverse situations.

Through the process of growing up, our children learn how to cope with life and problems. They develop either healthy or unhealthy coping skills.

Unhealthy Coping Skills

Unhealthy coping skills are developed when children encounter misleading situations as they grow. If children learn that life is out of their control, they also learn unhealthy ways of coping with the fear, anger and pain caused by not being able to make themselves happy. This most often takes the form of acting out / alcohol or drug abuse / passive behavior / changes in eating (anorexia or bulimia) or sleeping habits (insomnia or excessive sleeping) / personality swings / decline in work or school / inability to concentrate / loss of social contacts.

When self-destructive coping skills do not help children gain control over their lives (often they make things worse) children slip into helplessness and feel or think, "I can't change (the situation causing them pain), I need (something or someone outside of their control) to change things". From here, feelings of hopelessness may take over. "Things will never change. There's nothing I can do to escape this pain. This pain will go on for as long as I live". At this point, some children realize that there IS something they can do to escape the pain—that something is either to take drugs or alcohol to try to deaden the pain or to take their life.

How Children are Taught Unhealthy Coping Skills

The three major ways parents teach their children unhealthy coping skills are:

FIRST: Over-protecting their children (The "Permissive" Parenting Style). "Running interference" for a child by simply interfering with his life. Parents who are afraid of their children encountering pain and failure, step in and "solve" problems for their children. This behavior conveys three destructive messages to our children:

1. Life is supposed to be happy—it is not okay to have problems and if you do, you are a failure; after all, mom and dad never have problems.

2. I (the child) am incapable of handling problems. If I were capable, mom and dad would let me solve my own problems. Mom and dad know everything and they're telling me by their behavior that I will never be able to solve my own problems.

3. The world will ALWAYS care about me and rescue me.

SECOND: Some parents are not sure how to teach their children healthy coping skills.

THIRD: At the other extreme (The "Authoritarian" Parenting Style); parents convey either by words or actions, that their child can only be lovable if he is successful and never fails at anything. What happens when we expect too much of our children? They feel that they can only be loved and accepted by achieving. A life disappointment or rejection can translate into "I'm a failure, unlovable and unacceptable".

What Are Healthy Coping Skills?

Healthy coping skills are: knowing that we control our own lives: if we have a conflict or failure, we can change the situation. There is no such thing as a mistake. If we learn something from an experience, it is a lesson. If we can't get what we want, we can make a situation the best it can be. Sometimes we have to accept that a situation IS the best it can be, even if it means the acceptance of loss and the experience of pain. Pain is temporary; *pain passes with time.*

It is our job as parents to teach our children healthy coping skills. Unfortunately, in order for our children to learn healthy coping skills, they must encounter negative situations on their own and learn how to deal with them. We parents can do much to help our children learn healthy coping skills. We can act as support: endeavor to never solve their problems for them; give them permission to have feelings (by encouraging them to tell us what they feel); and ask questions: "What can you do about the problem? What did you do to create this situation? Help them know that they have control and only they can solve the problem by taking action in their own behalf.

How do we teach coping skills and control? We must step back and allow our children to make mistakes, hurt, and allow them to learn ways they can create a better situation for themselves. They must do this their way, not our way. We can help by constantly reflecting the situation back to them instead of giving them our knowledge gained from our experiences. We stop telling them what to do about a problem, or worse, doing something for them. We listen to their problem and ask, "What are you feeling about the situation? What are you going to do about it?" We ask, "What do you want from this situation? What are you willing to settle for in this situation?" and most important, help them see the consequences of their actions, how they created the situation and what the consequences are for the alternatives they propose. We support, we do not interfere.

33

How We Teach Children Healthy Coping Skills

Most of today's parents were raised by parents who structured, disciplined, and forced us to face the consequences of our actions in the same way the world does. When it came time for us to emancipate, the world and its demands were so similar to what was expected of us as children growing up, there was little or no shock at attaining adulthood.

Tragically, we parents often "run interference" for our children. What is running interference? It is when parents don't allow children to face the consequences of their actions. Parents who, for example, run to the school, neighbors or their kid's friends in order to "save" their children from situations the child has created, are running interference. Children interpret these behaviors by the parents as telling them; "You cannot take care of yourself. You will always need me to solve your problems." Many are deeply afraid that "we are trying to control them and their lives". This is part of the reason that our children "control battle" and "power struggle" with us. We can empathize that our goal is to teach them to be in better control. Once children realize that we truly want them to have control in their own life, our relationship with them shifts to a "win / win".

What happens when a parent doesn't help a child learn to resolve his own problems? What happens to a child who doesn't learn to "deal out" what's happening to him for his own self? Children may interpret our behavior as a message that they are incapable and will ALWAYS need to depend on someone else. There is a key theme here. It is "forever". While it is rarely verbalized, our children see things as "forever" until they have had enough experience with life to learn that nothing is forever. Coping skills and control teach our children that:

1) NOTHING is forever.
2) Failure is a way to learn.
3) ALL people make mistakes.
4) Pain, no matter how intense, is temporary.
5) "I can change my life and make it better for ME!"
   (not just for mom, dad or friends).

There is a balance in what we teach our children. This is true for under-achieving and over-achieving kids. We can love / help them in a way where they learn to love / help themselves. We can expect the best from our children while we let them know that we still respect them when they have a failure. Teaching our children coping skills is one of the greatest gifts we will ever give our children. So when they stumble on life's obstacles, they will be able to pick themselves up, dust themselves off and continue on; knowing, they are worthwhile and human.

Self Destructive Coping Skills

Acting out (Angry, impulsive, inappropriate behavior)
Alcohol or drug abuse
Passive behavior (withdrawn, lethargic)
Dramatic change in eating habits
Dramatic change in sleeping habits
Dramatic personality changes
Mood swings (from one extreme to the other)
Extreme decline in school (over a short period of time)
Inability to concentrate
Loss of friends, fear of peers (making friends)

Clues to Suicidal Thoughts

Excessive fear of change / separation
    (Grade School to Jr. High, Jr. High to High School,
    High School to College)
Helplessness
Hopelessness
Obsession with death (talking, thinking, writing)
Definite plan (making a will, giving away possessions)

Healthy Coping Skills

It is our job as parents to teach our children healthy coping skills. Unfortunately, in order for our children to learn healthy coping skills, they must encounter negative situations ON THEIR OWN and learn how to deal with them.

What Parents Can Do to Help:

Parents can be of the most value to our children if we act as a support to our children.

1. Never solve a problem for them.
2. Ask them questions: What did YOU do? What did YOU do to create this situation?
3. Help them know that THEY have control and only THEY can solve the problem by taking ACTION on their own behalf.

Chapter Two

How To Level With
Your Children

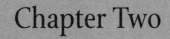

It's NOT impossible to be
consistent as a parent.

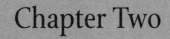

All you need is a little planning,
a little communication
and paper and pen.

The Three Major
Parts To Levelling

Combine any of the following and adapt them to your lifestyle.

House Rules:
Bottom line rules for the household, no matter what level the child is on, and privileges for each level.
Behavior:
Specific behavior, homework (study hall), automatic negative day behavior, and bonus points.
Chores:
Points earned according to how well chores are done, allowance deductions for waste, and clothing allowance.

*See Chapter Nine — Table of Contents

The next page tells you how to begin..

How To Begin

In Chapter Nine You Will Find:
• Hot Line phone number and address for questions.
• Sample Levels and Sample House Rules.
• Blank Levels and Blank House rules sheets.
• Two Sample Chore Lists (one simple and one more comprehensive).
• Two Blank Chore Lists (one simple and one more comprehensive).
• Sample and Blank Motivation Lists.
• Sample charts (Optional Memory Aid).
• Blank charts (Optional Memory Aid).
• A blank "budget" to help adolescents comprehend what emancipation entails.
• A sheet of Cartoon Awards to help motivate younger children.
• Three cut out "Notes" Sheets for making notes as you read.

Please Note:
I strongly suggest that you make and use only copies of the blank sheets. Before you start writing, make as many copies as you think you will need, so that you can change and update your Level System as you go.

What you will need to begin:
A pen or wordprocessor.
Colored marking pens (I suggest yellow, pink, and green).
Copies of the blank rules list, motivation list, chore list, and charts.

Levels and Days:
Under the Level Concept, a child must follow certain rules and depending on how well he follows the rules, may enjoy compensating privileges. This is achieved by having four levels from Level Zero to Level Three. On Level Zero, a child has no privileges, and graduating up level by level, achieves maximum privileges on Level Three.

Levelling offers you three kinds of days
"P" = Perfect
"+" = Acceptable
"-" = Negative

39

How It Works

For a child to advance a level, he must have seven "P" or perfect days in a row. If a child earns a "+" or acceptable day (two points less than the total points possible), he neither moves up or down. A "-" or negative day is earned when a child receives four points less than the total possible. If a child earns seven "-" or negative days in any three month period, he moves down a level. Every three months all "-" or negative days are wiped out, thus giving your child a fresh start.

You may wish to alter the set up of the number of "P", "+" and "-" days to suit your lifestyle and children. I have found, however, that this set up works well for children between ages 7 and 15. I suggest that if your children are in this age range, you begin with the system as outlined and alter it if you find a need. I have included additional information—Chapter Five (the separating adolescent) and Chapter Six (children under seven) which will help you set up Levelling for your older or younger children.

I recommend starting children on Level One if they are needing more structure at first. This way, there are consequences for poor behavior: moving down to Level Zero (having no privileges and freedom). If a child starts out on Level Zero, he has nothing to lose by manifesting the worst behavior he is capable of. If your child is functioning relatively well and used to more freedom, you can start your child on higher levels. If they need more structure, they will show you by their behavior where they developmentally need to be in the Level system. If your child stages a major rebellion after you begin Levelling, it is best to try to stick out the seven "-" days before moving him down. It is important for you to know that you can give a "-" for each time your child breaks a bottom line rule, such as disrespect. So if your child "out and out rebels" and keeps pushing you during that day, they can quickly move down to level zero. You are the final authority in your home, and, anytime, can override the Level system if you feel it is in the best interest of your child, your home, and your sanity. Be aware, though, that if you back off the agreed upon system, you will be giving your child the unspoken message that he doesn't have to take Levelling seriously. You will defeat the goal of giving your child the security of knowing what to expect and force yourself back into the role of having to reestablish your authority. I'll let you know here that without your "moral, loving authority", no method of parenting will ever be effective enough to adequately teach your children the values they need to best succeed in the world. This lack of firm, constant rules or laws is similar to having traffic laws "sometimes." Would you want to drive on the freeway without knowing if today is a "sometimes" day? Our children often determine if today is a "sometimes" day by testing us with their behavior. Once you have established a basic structure that you truly follow through with, I have found that it takes about eight weeks for most children to realize that their parents are serious and that it is time to learn to deal within reality. This is opposed to "La La land" that many teens would like to live in. This is a world where there are no rules, where they have all the rights and the parents all the responsibility.

You do have options other than overriding your Level system. A possession sweep, for example, can be very effective in getting your point across. In a possession sweep the parents go through the child's room and confiscate all "treasured" items: stereo, TV, special clothes, etc. Lock them away for a period of time or until the child has earned their return. Some parents use the confiscated items as rewards— handing them back one at a time for perfect days or special jobs done. Additionally, the Sample Motivation List included in Chapter Nine and Leverage in Parenting in the next section contains ideas which will "get your child's attention." One parent just threatens to take away her adolescent daughter's make-up and "instantly" has a cooperative child who minutes before was "making mom crazy."

In talks I give on Levelling, I've had parents question the concept of rewards and motivation. Ultimately, I wish for your children to contribute to the household because they "want to" and not for a reward. Realistically, human nature, to one extent or another, dictates that we must get something for our efforts. I ask the parents who question rewards if they would continue to work at their jobs if they didn't get paid. While this is a different situation, it is not so very different as we would believe. With children, we begin motivating them with rewards and consequences. Eventually, the feelings of ego strength and self-worth become the "reward." If you analyze adult life, we are motivated by rewards, consequences, feelings of self-worth or ego strength gained from our actions and accomplishments.

Leverage in Parenting

Before you begin to set up your rules and levels, break out of your usual thoughts on consequences for your children. Leverage is knowing what resources you possess which will influence another person to work towards goals with you. We cannot control our children. They are busy proving that to us all the time! However, we do have the power to steer and influence them. In any relationship, when we have something that someone else needs or wants, it gives us power in their lives. Our children want many things from us. Sometimes it's: "Buy Me, Take Me, Do Me and Give Me". So, the good news, is that you have much power and leverage in teaching your children. The point to disciplining children is not to punish but to teach them the skills and values necessary for their successful functioning in the world. Leverage in conjunction with a level system is knowing what really motivates your children. Please turn to the sample and blank Motivation List on pages 132 and 133 in Chapter Nine. Start with a list of positive motivators, then create a list of consequences (punishments) for each of your children. Think of the things each child likes the best and dislikes the most. Next, cross off anything which is a punishment to you, the parent. Even though you know that a payoff or consequence will work better for Johnny than for your daughter Jenny, include it in the system as a consequence or payoff for both children. A set of rules for each child is best avoided and should only be used if there is a great age discrepancy between your children, thus avoiding complaints about "special treatment" for siblings.

Take your lists of consequences and payoffs (what motivates Johnny and Jenny) and combine them to make a motivation list for all of your children. If you find yourself struggling with deciding what to put on the list, remember that you are striving to motivate your children without punishing yourself. A few examples are: taking away stereos, TV, make-up, curling irons, telephone—I think you get the idea. I know of one parent who could not get her son to stay in his room. When sent there he would slip out the window. She removed all of his pants from his room and never had a problem with his slipping out again! Use your Motivation List to help you set up your house rules and levels.

To further illustrate the concept of motivating children, I will tell you of a parent who abandoned her system because her child's consequences were a punishment for her. This mother owns her own business and works at home. When her son broke the rules, she would send him to his room while she continued to work in her office (located in the basement). Instead of sitting quietly in his room, he played, made a mess, or sneaked downstairs to the first level of the house.

In an attempt to gain control, the mother had him sit in a chair in her office where he wiggled, cried, talked and disturbed her while she tried to run her business. She abandoned her Levelling system and her son went back to worse behavior, which he had exhibited before she had set Levelling up.

Finally, she called our hot line and asked what to do. We asked her what her son hated the most and her answer was, "Being alone and left out of things; that's why I was sending him to his room!" Because she couldn't stop work and oversee him while he was in his room, this was a consequence which punished the parent, eventually causing her to abandon Levelling. I suggested that when her son broke a bottom line rule, she not send him immediately to his room, but wait until evening when Daddy was home and everyone was talking and sharing and having a good time. This way she could oversee his consequence without disrupting the running of her business. Her son hated being left out of "family time." She added this consequence to her system and now is able to attend to her business duties without distraction and aggravation from her son.

For parents, Levelling was created to make your life easier while raising responsible, caring children into adulthood. If Levelling does not create a harmoniously functioning family unit, you will never follow through with the payoffs and consequences you have established for your children and you will end up defeating the system before you begin.

For children, Levelling was created not only to resolve problems. It also creates the stability in the home environment which gives children the security and bonding they carry with them for the rest of their lives.

There is a great difference between controlling and helping others. Often the difference is lost with parents—when children are young and helpless, we must control for their own safety. As children grow, we often control, thinking we are supporting.

Responsibility For...

**When I feel responsible FOR others,
I am really trying to CONTROL them...**

I:

Fix

Protect

Rescue

Control

Carry their feelings

Don't listen

I feel:

Tired

Anxious

Fearful

Liable

I am concerned with:

The solution

Answers

Circumstances

Being right

Details

Performance

I become a negative manipulator.

I expect the person to live up to my expectations.

Anonymous

Parenting Styles...

Authoritarian Parent

•

Highly Structured

•

Over-Controlling

•

Child not taught to make decisions for self

Permissive Parent

Helicopter Parent

•

Parent "fixes" / "runs interference"

•

Does for the child

•

Child does not learn to do for self

Coach

the best

•

Assertive

•

Compassionate

•

Structures a "learning environment"

•

Follows through with consequences

•

Believes in the child's ability to learn

4 Things Kids Need Most

1. Unconditional Love that lets your child know they're loved, no matter what.

2. "Active Listening" to your child's feelings without judgement. Agree to disagree, when your opinions differ.

3. Do Not "run interference" for them. Teach them the coping skills to gain control of their own life.

4. A "Total Learning Environment" with clear expectations and consequences so they can WIN at the "responsibility game."

Charting

Why a Chart? In home testing it has been found that a chart offers a memory aid for both the parents and child. The charts contained in Chapter Nine are optional; Levelling will work with or without them. However, I have found them to be a tremendous help in keeping track of how my children are doing. Charts make it easier for children to determine what level they are on and how many positive and negative days they have.

I have supplied blank charts to help you set up your own. I strongly urge that you make copies of the blank charts before you start filling them in so you have the option of changing the system as your children grow. You may also find it useful to make copies of your charts after you have decided on headings and sections so that you do not have to fill in the headings and sections each month.

The samples in Chapter Nine were set up for two children, ages 11 and 14. If you have children younger than 7 or older than 16, you will find special chapters toward the end of this book titled; "The Separating Adolescent — Level Four" and "Levelling With Children Under Seven" written to give you suggestions for adapting the system for younger and older children. Remember that the hotline number and address are included in Chapter Nine for additional resources or advice.

I found it helpful to keep the filled-in Motivation List at hand while setting up the charting system.

If you choose to use charts, you will need to decide where to keep them. I suggest that you:

- Post (perhaps on your refrigerator.)

- Distribute copies to your children. (This works well, although I did find that some children "lost" their copies, giving them an excuse not to do their chores, etc. When I started charging $1.00 per replacement copy, the problem was quickly eliminated.)

- Keep in a folder accessible to your children.

Chapter Three

LEVEL, RULES AND
BEHAVIOR

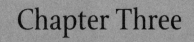

Our children WANT to feel
good and successful.

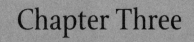

Children have repeatedly said what
they love about *Levelling* is that the
"rules don't keep changing."

Determining Levels and Rules

Please refer to your copies of the pages titled "Levels and House Rules" from Chapter Nine. You have one blank and one sample "Levels and House Rules" sheet.

Bottom Line rules are at the top of the page. These are rules which, if broken, constitute an automatic negative day. Remember that, in the sample, seven "-" days in a three month period and the child moves down a level. Be sure to remind your child when he's getting close to going up or down a level.

You do need "Bottom Line" rules for the household. Bottom line rules are those behaviors that will absolutely not be tolerated. They are the "No No's". You only have so much time and energy. Any one child has more time and energy than you or you and your spouse. So it is important to "pick your battles". These are the more serious lines that you want to stand behind with the time and energy that you have. Try not to load up the bottom line rules with things which are annoying but tolerable. Use the levels to deal with less serious behaviors. Check your Motivation List, select, and write in your privileges, freedoms and consequences for each level. Beyond these guidelines, let your lifestyle dictate what is important to you and your children!

I suggest that each child receive a copy of the Levels and House Rules or that they be posted in a place where the children can have easy access to them.

I encourage you to:

Let your child participate in setting up the "game" by sitting down with them and, as a family, decide what the rules, benefits, and restrictions will be for each level. Remember, you are the parents. You support the household and have the ultimate authority to decide what will be or will not be for each level.

Add to and modify the system as new situations come up. Do not be afraid to tell your children, "I'm writing a new rule, so you might want to read it."

Responsibility To...

**When I feel responsible TO others,
I am trying to HELP instead of control them**

I:
Show empathy
Encourage
Share my experiences
Confront
Level
Am sensitive
Listen

I feel:
Relaxed
Free
Aware
High self-esteem

I am concerned with:
Relating person to person
Feelings
The person

I believe that if I share myself, the other
person has enough to make it.

I expect the person to be responsible for
himself and his own actions.

I can trust and let go.

I am a helper / guide.

Anonymous

Charting and Tracking

Depending on the age of your children and your situation, you may want to just add on to the sample Levels and House Rules which I have supplied; or adopt the theory, and start from scratch. Remember the hotline phone number and address in Chapter Nine if you have questions or want support on things as they arise.

Begin by writing or typing in the consequences and privileges you have decided upon on your copied originals of the Blank "Levels and House Rules" (see Chapter Nine, page 130).

Tracking Behavior

Please refer to the "Sample Behavior Chart" in Chapter Nine, page 140. You will be using your copies of the "Blank Behavior Chart" from Chapter Nine, page 141.

1. Start by filling in your copy of the "Blank Behavior Chart" with the child's name and the month you are working with. Each child in your family will need his own Behavior Chart.

2. Next, decide on headings. The headings that worked best for me were:
    - Homework
    - Behavior
    - Bonuses
    - Automatic Negative Day

Make headings of those things you want your child to do or to not do. Again, the beauty of Levelling is that you may decide what fits your household—be creative!

After filling in your headings, your Behavior Chart should look similar to the following sample Behavior Chart.

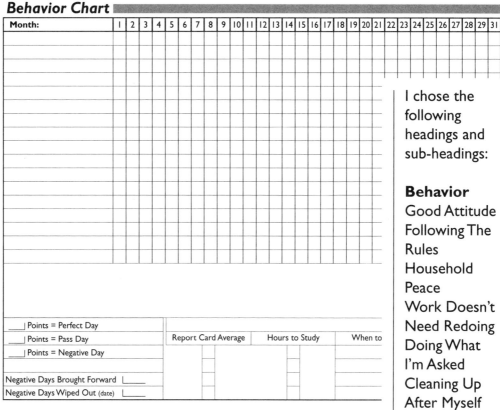

Behavior Chart

Month:	1	2	3	4	5	6	7	8	9	10	11	12	13	14	15	16	17	18	19	20	21	22	23	24	25	26	27	28	29	30	31

____| Points = Perfect Day
____| Points = Pass Day
____| Points = Negative Day

Negative Days Brought Forward |____
Negative Days Wiped Out (date) |____

Report Card Average	Hours to Study	When to

I chose the following headings and sub-headings:

Behavior
Good Attitude
Following The Rules
Household Peace
Work Doesn't Need Redoing
Doing What I'm Asked
Cleaning Up After Myself

Bonuses
Helping Points
Listening Points

Automatic Negative Day
Disrespect
Didn't Heed Warning
Breaking Grounding
Not Going to Time Out

3. After determining your headings, decide what sections or behaviors are important to your children and yourself. List them under headings. (See Sample Behavior Chart in Chapter Nine.)

After filling in your sections, your Behavior Chart should look something like the following:

Behavior Chart

Month:	1	2	3	4	5	6	7	8	9	10	11	12	13	14	15	16	17	18	19	20	21	22	23	24	25	26	27	28	29	30	31
Homework:																															
Behavior:																															
Good Attitude																															
Household Peace																															
Doing What I'm Asked																															
Following the Rules																															
Work Doesn't Need Redoing																															
Clean Up After Myself																															
Bonuses:																															
Helping Points																															
Listening Points																															
Automatic Negative Day:																															
Disrespect																															
Breaking Grounding																															
Lying																															
Didn't Heed Warning																															
Not Going to Time Out																															
Not Doing Chores At All																															
Daily Total Due:																															

____| Points = Perfect Day
____| Points = Pass Day
____| Points = Negative Day

Negative Days Brought Forward |____
Negative Days Wiped Out (date) |____

Report Card Average	Hours to Study	When to Study
B		
C		
D		
F		

Homework was very important to me, so I gave it a heading all to itself. I gave bonuses for helping and listening. All of the "Bottom Line" rules from the House Rules went under the Automatic Negative Day heading. I will discuss chores in the next section. If you find that you have more headings and sub-headings than there is room for on the blank chart provided, just continue another chart. If you do run out of room on the chart provided, you may wish to reconsider the importance of each heading and sub-heading with an eye to eliminating some of the headings or sub-headings prior to starting a second chart. It is easier for you and your children if the system is kept as simple as possible.

Next, you must decide on a point value for each section. You are setting up your own system so make modifications that fit your home. Let the importance of each item determine the point value. A rule of thumb is to assign a five to the most important item(s), a one to the least important item(s) and assign four(s) three(s) and two(s) to the balance of your items based on their importance.

Remember that, in the examples, there are only two points between a perfect day and a "+ day" and four points between a perfect day and a "- day." In the first sample chart, the child can have a "+ day" even if they don't do their homework. This is accomplished by getting bonus points for helping and listening, thereby not risking going down a level. They would not, however, be able to have a perfect day (7 perfect days to move up a level) unless the homework was done. I did this deliberately. The child could rebel by not doing his homework, and take the consequences (perhaps ruining a string of "perfect days") or the alternate consequence of getting a "- day" if he did not earn the bonus points for helping and listening in addition to not doing his homework. Children are going to rebel. There's no getting around it. Structure your Level System so that your children can rebel on behaviors and issues which you consider to be the least important by giving a smaller point value to these issues. Thus, your children will rebel on the issues of lesser consequence because the consequences of rebelling on issues you find most important are too great.

I suggest that you keep bonus points as a legitimate "bonus" and do not include them in the "Daily Point Total." Add them in after you total for the day; i.e., you have a "- day" but after we add in your bonus points, you have a "+ day." This allows your children to "slip" on bonus behavior and still get a perfect day or a "+ day." Bonus points are the child's "redemption" and a way for you to be a "good guy" in the coaching process with your children.

If you decide to include chores in your Level System, they should be included in the "Daily Point Total." The bonus points are not included in the "Daily Points" so it is possible for the child to rebel to a certain degree, and still get a "+ day" or a "P day."

On the Sample Behavior Chart in Chapter Nine there are 16 Daily Points possible, including chores and excluding bonus points if you add:

Homework = 5 points

Behavior = 6 total points possible

Chores = 5 total points possible (see Sample Chore Chart, page 138)

Total = 16 Total possible points

After assigning the points to the sub-headings, total up the maximum points possible (excluding the bonus points) to arrive at the total for a "P day"—in the example, a total of 16. Next, decide how many points constitute a "+ day." In the example, 13 is the high for a "+ day." Thus, there is a two point spread between a "P day" and a "+ day." I set it up this way because the child must do all of the "high point" or important sections in order to get a "P day" and yet he may slip or rebel on the "low point" or less important sub-headings and still receive a "P day" by receiving bonus points. Therefore, in the example:

15 to 16 points = A Perfect Day.
Figuring a "P day" spread automatically gives you the high number for a "+ day"—in the example, 13 points. I suggest that you use the same point spread between a "+ day" and a "- day" for the reasons stated earlier. Thus, in the example:

13 to 14 points = a "+ day" and 12 and below = a "- day." Remember that homework was important enough to merit a heading all to itself? Homework = 5 points. If the child, in the example, does not do his homework, but earns both bonus points:

16-5=11 points, +2 bonus points, he will receive 13 points for a "+ day."

Once again, if there is an issue at your house that is crucial, it will help to assign that issue or sub-heading a large point value, and structure your system to allow the child to rebel on minor issues rather than major issues within the system. Be sure that it is not possible for the child to rebel on crucial issues and still earn a perfect day.

As an extra incentive, I allowed the children to use their bonus points to "buy" extra privileges or they may have the points added to their daily total, if they wished. (See page 57 for a further explanation.)

After you have decided on the point value for each behavior, fill in the boxes with the points so your chart is complete. See Chapter Nine, page 140 for an example. As you can see, the line "Homework" is followed by a "5", (which is the chosen point value), in each of the boxes corresponding/under each day of the month (1 to 31). The next line down contains the Heading "Behavior." The next line down contains the sub-heading "good attitude" followed by a "1," (which is the chosen point value), in each of the boxes corresponding/under each day of the month. (1 to 31).

While your Behavior Chart will probably have different headings of your choosing, after you finish filling in your Behavior Chart it will look very much like our example. At this point, before you write in the current month, you will find it helpful to make copies of your Behavior Chart so that you will not have to fill in a blank chart each month. If you do make copies after you have filled in this information, you will need only to write in the name of the current month and update the miscellaneous information at the bottom of the chart (negative days brought forward) in order to be set up for each new month.

Token Slips

As I mentioned, I have found that trading bonus points for Token Slips can be very helpful. It can solve many problems and end some of the familiar unhappy refrains which parents often hear. One problem Token Slips solves is keeping a child motivated to get the "Bonus Points" even if he already has a perfect day. For example, your child might choose to "buy" a ride to the movies rather than use his bonus points to make a "- day" into a "+ day" or a "+ day" into a "P day". If he already has a "P day," you can also trade token slips for favors. This works wonderfully to stop the "you never" and "everyone else's parents always."

When you ask your child to do something for you (run an errand, get a cup of coffee, or a Coke for you, etc.), you assign the favor a Token Slip (TS) value. For example, a cup of coffee is worth 1 TS. When the child brings you the coffee he also brings a pencil and paper. You write the value ("1" in this case) and give it to your child. He can use the token slips for rides, special privileges, return favors from you, etc. This quickly puts an end to the "you don't care, you never do anything for me" refrain. My children fight over who gets to prepare and serve Sunday morning breakfast in bed to us for a five point TS. They must, however, clean up the kitchen and wash the dishes before getting "paid". TS's really help moms who feel over-used by children's demands. They even things up a bit. Last, I have tried using buttons instead of paper and abandoned them when one child found where the buttons were kept and used them as unearned tokens.

Using Your Behavior Chart

As the day progresses, or at the end of the day, mark off, in green, the areas where your child does not "make the grade." Mark over the number, located in the box under the day and next to the section which corresponds to the behavior in question. If, for example, on the third day of the month, your child fought with his sister, you would mark in green, over the "1", in the box on the line, "Household Peace" and in the column under 3 (the third day of the current month). Marking in color makes it very easy to see. At the end of the day a child will have: one or no green marks = a perfect day; two or three green marks = a "+ day"; more than three green marks = a "- day."

Behavior Chart

Month: January	1	2	3	4	5	6	7	8	9	10	11	12
Homework:												
Behavior:												
Good Attitude												
Household Peace	1	1	■	1	1	1	1	1	1	1	1	1
Doing What I'm Asked												

To Total Your Behavior Chart

In the column for the current day, total all green marks above the "Bonuses" line, and deduct this amount from the total possible points for the day. (In the sample this is 11 possible points if chores are not included.)

If your child chooses, add any bonus points earned to the total. (In the sample this would add a possible two points to the "Daily Points.")

Example: If your child as three green marks in the column for the current day and has earned one bonus point for the current day and wishes to add this to his "Daily Point Total," your calculations would be:

11 possible points
-3 green marks
_____

=8 points
+1 bonus point
_____

=9 points for the Daily Point Total or a "+ day."

After adding up the total points for the day (Daily Point Total), check to see if there are any green marks under the "Automatic Negative Day" heading, and mark the "Daily Total Due" box with a:

- Yellow marker for a "P day" (perfect day)—11 to 10 points in the example,
- Pink marker for a "+ day" (plus day)—9 to 8 points in the example, or
- Green marker for a "- day" (negative day)—7 or fewer points in the example.

By using colored markers, it is very easy to see at a glance if your child is close to moving up a level (in the example, 7 perfect or yellow days in a row) or down a level (in the example, 7 green or "- days" in a three month period.)

Study Hall

At the bottom of the Behavior Chart is an area for study hall. In the sample, depending on the child's report card average, each child with an average below an "A" is expected to read or study during study hall even if they don't have homework. Remember that Levelling is set up to fit YOUR lifestyle and priorities. Change the examples so that they feel comfortable for you and your children.

Time Out

Time out is a very important part of Levelling. It is vital, however, that time out be used properly.

Time out is not a punishment. It is designed to give your child a chance to "cool down." When you or your child becomes too upset to function rationally, time out is called.

When time out is called on a younger child, the child sits in a chair so that he is looking at the wall, and is still "in the center of the action"—a family room perhaps. I like a chair because it makes the process safe, simple and structured. I worry about sending a child to his room when he is out of control. A chair in the room, where we are, allows us to better monitor our children. A child gets three time outs per day for 10 minutes each time. If he is still unable to talk to you rationally after three time outs, he is sent to his room for a fourth time out. This is an extended period of time; the rest of the evening, for example. When your child becomes too old to sit in a chair, I suggest you follow the same formula but separate yourself from your child by going into another room. I have found it best that your child not be allowed to watch TV or otherwise be distracted while in time out. The point of time out is designed to get things back into perspective and decide upon a better way to communicate. This is difficult to accomplish when distracted.

Very young children (ages 3-5) need more time outs with which to learn. For them, I suggest three time outs in the morning, three time outs in the afternoon and three time outs in the evening. The fourth time out would then be for the rest of the morning, afternoon or evening. I would suggest each time out to last only 3 minutes (an egg timer works well to remind you both when 3 minutes are up). At first, you may need to sit with your child on your lap to teach them how to deep breath and relax muscles. You might teach your child to have his head talk to his heart so that he can learn to relax and be a good boss for himself. There are wonderful relaxation tapes that can be used for children to help them relax on their own.

For a child of any age to resume interaction with the family after time out is completed, he must first be able to interact calmly with you. The suggested dialogue would go something as follows:

"Johnny, are you ready to talk?"
"Yes."
"Why were you sent to time out?"
"Because I kept yelling after you asked me not to."
"What could you do next time so you don't have to go to time out?"
"Yell outside."
"You know you lost a bonus "Listening Point" for not listening when I asked you to be quiet."
"Yes."
"Are you ready to rejoin the family?"
"Yes."

If the child is not ready to talk, or responds with hostility or sarcasm, the second, third, or fourth time out begins. It is important that you do ask the questions and that the child answers them calmly before he is allowed out of time out.

One reason to have the child at the "center of the action", (other than keeping an eye on him) is that a wonderful motivator for gaining your child's cooperation is to have your child witness family life going on without him. Many parents distribute hugs, pass out cookies or call for a "game night". The parent gives the rest of the family enough positive attention for the child in time out to be really motivated to rejoin the fun.

Here are the questions to be asked before a child is allowed out of time out:

1. Are you ready to talk?
2. Why were you timed out?
3. What could you do differently next time?

The consequences for your behavior this time are
_____. (Where applicable.)
4. Are you ready to rejoin the family now?

The suggested response when a child runs headlong into the system is, "No problem! If you do..., the reward is..., If you do..., the consequences are... The choice is up to you."

A child may time himself out, but to prevent him from timing himself out to get out of work, etc., this must count as one of the three time outs. Occasionally, the kids have "timed me out." If I'm having a particularly bad day, they have "suggested" that I could use some time to get myself together. This is perfectly valid. Time out works both ways.

Parents who have children who refuse to go to time out have asked me what to do. First, stay calm. If you can remain calm enough, you can end this dilemma permanently. Our children exhibit this behavior to get attention. I have found that if I completely ignore a child who won't go to time out, I quickly obtain his cooperation. Pretend that your child is not in the house. Do not tell him what you are doing. Wait for him to notice that he has ceased to exist as far as you're concerned and asks you what's going on. Then, simply and CALMLY tell him that you will not talk to him until he has gone to time out. He may escalate in order to get you to respond. REMAIN CALM and continue to ignore him. Turn on the TV, radio, start a project, or go to your room and close the door. If he is older, leave the house. If he puts you in a situation where you must respond; throwing toys for example, remove the toys without words or emotions. Wait for him to understand that he will not get what he wants if he won't follow the rules. You can do what I call a "ROOM SWEEP" by taking all toys (all valuable items for the older children). They can be locked away until your child is following the rules; such as following the time out procedure appropriately. The child can earn the items back as they show they are willing to respect you and work with the basic rules. I'll reiterate that if you do not have the power as the parent, with the ultimate authority to teach safe limits, no strategy you use will be quite enough to teach your children the responsibility and values they need to best succeed in a world of relationships.

Negative Attention Syndrome

Levelling is particularly effective with children who have gotten into the "Negative Attention Syndrome." To deal with children who are into the habit of getting attention for acting out, make sure that you first make it totally clear that you will not be giving your child attention for negative behavior. This is really critical. Be sure you TELL your child what you are doing! He has learned that the way to get attention from you is to misbehave. If you stop responding to him, his logical choice is to escalate his negative behavior.

You must make it perfectly clear that you will no longer pay attention to him when he is being obnoxious, and give him very clear, positive examples of what he CAN do to get your attention. As difficult as it may be to believe at times, it will help to keep in mind that your child really does want your love and attention. You taught him that he could get your attention by misbehaving, and with a little patience, you can teach him to get love and attention in a good, healthy, positive manner.

Your conversation with your child might go something like this:

"Johnny, I know that you think the only way you can get my attention is to misbehave."(Never say "be bad" because Johnny will believe that he is bad instead of understanding that it is his behavior that is unacceptable.)

"I'm tired of your behavior and have decided not to give you attention when you don't behave properly. It makes me unhappy when you do things like _____. I have decided that I'll only give you attention when you behave in a positive manner like _____."

Follow this up with abundant praise whenever he behaves properly. Tell him each time he misbehaves that:

"I don't like your behavior (state what the behavior in question is and what he could have done that would have been more positive). I don't want to talk to or be around you right now. Just like you, I don't like being around people when they are doing things which make me unhappy. I love you, so I'll get over being unhappy with you. In 10 to 15 minutes I'll feel like being around you again."

Don't forget that time out can be a very useful tool when your child is pushing to get negative attention. Please be aware that, as your child's behavior changes, it is easy to forget to reinforce his positive behavior. It is critically important that you follow up and keep praising him so he won't revert to negative behavior to get attention.

Tantrums Need An Audience

Dear Old Mom!

How foolish are we Mothers,
Who carry life so dear.
There are a thousand things
Which each of us do fear.

We fear our children growing,
Yet punish them for not.
What is a spilled mess
But a forgettable blot.

Our children must be "normal,"
And yet they must excel.
I really think we Mothers
Are truly just not well!

Bless our young one's hearts,
For all this, they do try.
Oh, they will never know
The how & when & why.

That they'll never be "good
enough"
Never will succeed,
In pleasing "dear old Mom,"
Whose heart will always bleed.

For, we don't understand,
That what we fear is this:
The pain involved in growing
Is what we wish they'd miss!

We all must learn the hard way.
It's tears which make us grow.
So, poor old Mom, she suffers,
And tries to make it not so!

Mom

Chapter Four

CHORES

❖

Some parents maintain that a child
will, soon enough, have to work.

❖

They feel asking a child to help with
housework is shortening their childhood.

❖

These parents forget that we obtain our
ego strength from what we can do
and accomplish.

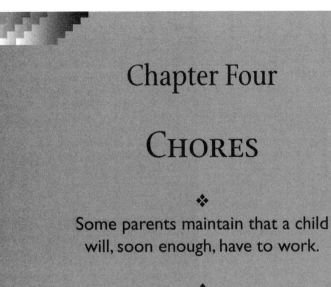

Chores

Chores are not a necessary part of the Levelling System. You may decide not to involve your child in the household routine. However, I feel so strongly about chores being good for children that I have not only included chores in this book, but encourage you to understand how they can benefit your child. No matter what the age of the child or adult, we gain ego strength from being able to "do things." Doing helps us to identify ourselves.

Chores teach children the ego strength gained from "knowing I can do". They learn the moral value that; in order to take from the world, they must also give. Chores teach children how to care for themselves as they grow. When chores are tied into their allowance, they see that they have control over their own finances. Good reality testing is discovered when "pay" is proportionate to "doing" and "how well" the job is done. This, in our opinion, is good preparation for emancipation-when the child leaves home. Children who do not do chores or contribute to the household find it very painful to learn these activities when they leave home and face the world on their own.

Many households have used chores to prepare their children for the jobs they will eventually hold. We can explain to children how, if they were employed outside of the home, they could be fired for doing that kind of job. We can go on to explain what a future boss might require. For teenage boys, letting them know we are trying to teach them to be men, helps. I've never seen a teenage boy respond with: "I don't want to be a man".

I used chores to give the children the opportunity to contribute to the household, earn spending money, and earn bonus money which they spent in any fashion they desired.

While parental demands of children is an extremely personal topic, I would like to share my own views on household chores. Children gain self-esteem from their accomplishments. Chores are a great way for a child to display his abilities and also make a contribution to the household. Parenting is perhaps the strangest of all investments. We spend hundreds of thousands of dollars and enormous time and energy, in an effort to help our children leave us. Ideally, we train our children to walk from our home and establish a happy, successful life. As strange as this job description may seem, it is the job we accept when we take the responsibility of parenting a child.

In many cases, parents choose not to ask their children to contribute to the household by doing chores. While this is a decision which has no right or wrong answer, we must, as good parents, train our children to care for themselves and their environment after they leave us. We have all heard the jokes about children sending their laundry home or the newlywed who burned water. Perhaps you were one of these unfortunate young adults yourself. A loving a conscientious parent foresees the stress created by "moving away from home" and best prepares their child. Life is eased by having the knowledge that we can take care of ourselves. Thus, our child won't have to ask others or "learn the hard way in a hurry." Because doing chores enhances a child's self-esteem and allows him to contribute to the environment which nurtures him, I believe that having a child do chores is a wise choice. In my household, the children understand that some of their chores are a "contribution," and some are done so that they can earn spending money. I pay the children as an employer might, thus preparing them for the world of employment. Since they earn their own money, they also have the choice to spend it in any way they wish. I also have "rotated" the chores so that each child has mastered each aspect of caring for a home; from cooking and cleaning to laundry.

Parents often ask what they should expect from their children at a given age. I am including the basic developmental stages along with the general ages at which chores and responsibilities may be assigned. I hope this gives you an overall view of what to expect from your child at any point in his development.

Developmental Stages

1 to 2 years:

During this period it is normal for a child to become afraid when his parents leave. This is a sign of the child's realization that he is separate from Mom and Dad. The fear is simply, "If Mom and Dad aren't part of me, they might leave and never come back." This stage normally fades as a child approaches 3 years. Parents can help their child through this stage by reassuring the child that they will return. It is helpful to give the child a specified time so that the child can learn to trust that the parent will return. Since a child this age has no time concept, the return time can be conveyed by concepts the child is able to understand: after lunch, after you go to sleep tonight, or after a TV show which is normally viewed. It is important that the parent does leave and not give in to the child's fears. Your child can only learn to trust you if you give him the opportunity to learn that you will be back at the time you said you would.

A child this age can be asked to follow simple directions, imitate housework, take his clothes off, bring and take objects places and pick up toys.

2 to 3 years:

The power struggles evident at this age may entail your child displaying temper tantrums complete with banging of head and feet on the floor. While this is a normal stage, it often succeeds in destroying a parent's serenity. REMEMBER, a tantrum must have an audience. If you leave the room, your child will quickly learn that tantrums aren't worth the energy. Your child will have a working vocabulary of 300-900 words during this stage and will understand between 2 and 3 thousand words. He will also understand time words i.e. morning or afternoon. You can use time out by sending him to a comfortable chair in order to "find his happy heart." Your child will seek and follow simple advice on tasks, play with peers, and enjoy putting one thing inside the other. He will be able to feed himself, put on his clothes, button large buttons, show an improving capacity for self-control and structure. Your child will start to remember "constant" rules like brushing his teeth before bed.

At this age, you can expect your child to: put toys away in the proper places and put his clothes away in his drawers. He may not get the correct drawer and may unfold clothes as he puts them away, but will enjoy the feelings of being "grown up" from this activity.

3 to 4 years:

This period ushers in the denial of emotions along with displays of empathy. Your child may begin lying because he sees himself as a "good" and "bad" self. When his "good" self says, "I didn't do it," he's really saying, "My bad self did it and since I'm being my good self right now, I didn't do it." Your child will probably also show a compulsion for "excessive" tidiness during this period.

At this age your child can: Garden, dust, wash hands, brush teeth, make his bed, set and clear the table, clean his room.

4 to 5 years:

Your child will now understand time concepts and have the ability to recognize good and bad behavior in himself and others. He can prepare dry cereal, tie his shoes, and bathe himself with assistance. Questions constitute between 15% and 25% of his speech. You can survive the questions by reminding yourself that this too is temporary and he will outgrow it.

During this period your child will be able to: put his toys away neatly where they belong, fold towels, empty unbreakables from the dishwasher, sweep (somewhat) the floor or walks.

5 to 6 years:

At this age, your child will normally start showing competitiveness with siblings or peers and begin relying on adult limit-setting for security.

Your child should be able to: handle liquids in the kitchen (milk, etc.) and make a sandwich. This is an age where your child can: run simple errands, answer the phone and convey a simple message, dress without assistance (though you may not agree with his choices) and bathe himself with the bathroom door open with your supervision.

6 to 7 years:

Your child should begin to understand cause and effect. He will be able to: fold and put away laundry, load and unload the dishwasher, dust, and take out the trash.

8 to 9 years:

Your child is now old enough to: vacuum, clean windows and mirrors, wash dishes, mop floors, clean the bathroom, edge the lawn, pull weeds, feed pets, and change the sheets on beds.

10 to 11 years:

Your child should be ready to do "light" cooking and baking with supervision and help, wash laundry, organize (clean garage, drawers, etc.), clean the refrigerator and clean the car.

12 to 13 years:

Your child can now: clean up after pets, wax floors, iron, and shovel snow.

He will also begin to express an interest in wearing "what everyone else is wearing." If your child badgers you for the expensive and "junk" clothing presently in vogue, a different approach is provided in the section on Clothing Allowance at the end of this chapter.

13 to 18 years:

During this period your child will be questioning the values and roles he learned from you in an effort to identify himself as separate and "adult." He will look outside of the home for people and ideas to have faith in. His worst fears will stem from possible ridicule or looking foolish in the eyes of his peers. In his need to separate from you, he will look to his peers to fulfill his need for closeness and acceptance.

I have presented possibilities for chores and responsibilities at the earliest suggested age. Please do not expect that your child will be able to do these things perfectly the first time.

As with all things, your child needs your help to teach him to do the job well. Help your child by challenging him to do the best he can. Remember, your criticisms, support and praise are being translated into how "good" or "bad" a person he feels he is.

Chore List

If you opt for chores, set up a Chore List (similar to the House Rules List) for each child. Make sure that you write down each part of the job that must be done so the child doesn't say, "I didn't know that was part of the job". This chore list will also act as an aid when you check chores.

Please refer to the Chore Charts in Chapter Nine. You will be using your own copies of the Simple Chore Chart (blank) or the Comprehesive Chore Chart (blank).

Johnny's Chores

Monday:
- Kitchen table-clear and rinse dinner dishes.
- Place in correct spot in dishwasher.
- Wipe table with a sponge-crumbs are wiped into your hand and rinsed down the sink. Crumbs are not wiped on the floor.
- Shake placemats over the sink and put back on the table.
- If placemats are soiled, put them in the laundry and put a clean set on the table.

Tuesday:
- Clean kitchen cupboard-ask which cupboard to clean.
- Take all things out of the cupboard.
- With soap and water and a clean rag, wipe down all surfaces of the cupboard.
- Place all items removed from the cupboard neatly back in the cupboard.

Wednesday:
- Change your sheets-remove dirty sheets and place them in the dirty clothes hamper in the basement.
- Get clean sheets and pillow case and make your bed with them.
- Be sure to tuck in all edges except the top edge.
- Put blankets on bed and tuck in the same as the top sheet.
- Put bedspread on neatly.
- Put clean pillow cases on pillows and fold under the bedspread.

Chore Tracking

If you have decided not to include chores in your Levelling system, you can proceed directly to page 92.

There are two Sample Chore Charts included in Chapter Nine. The first, on page 136 of Chapter Nine is a simplified chore tracking chart. The second, on page 138 is a more sophisticated tracking chart which would help you to include more options in dealing with your children's behaviors.

The second chore chart titled, "Comprehensive Chore Chart" presents greater detail. It includes a chart for chores, allowance, and a system to reduce wasted electricity, water and food. In this chart, chores do two things:

1) Earn points to be added to the behavior chart which are counted as part of the "Daily Total," (determining if the day was a "P day" a "+ day" or a "- day")

2) Earn money for allowance.

If you feel your child is too young for such detail, or if you want to simplify things, list the child's chores directly on the Behavior Chart. Assign each chore a point value and/or a monetary value. Remember, you can change the system later and go into a more detailed or simplified system if you wish.

The Comprehensive Chore Chart Sample gives the specific amounts of money and points it is possible for a child to earn. Allowance (or the amount a child earns for work done) is graduated and depends on what level the child is on (a child on Level three or four earns more for his chores than a child on level one or two). Allowance also fluctuates based on how well the child does his chores. The Chore List (page 73) details the chores which the child needs to do each day. The chore Chart is like a report card for the day's accomplishments.

ALL of the chores on the child's list for that day must be done, and done right, to earn the maximum allowance and points for the day. A child will earn more money for the same chores if he is on Level Three or Four than if he is on Level One or Two. This gives added incentive to achieve and remain on Level Three or Four. Please note that on Level

One and Two, if chores are done minimally, no money is earned. In the sample, at Level Three or Four, 20 cents per day minimum is payable for the poorest of jobs done.

As with the Behavior Chart, fill in the child's name and the month you are working on (each child will have his own Chore Chart).

Then, decide the maximum allowance you feel comfortable having your child earn each week. Divide this amount by seven (There are seven days in each week). Write this amount in the box directly under the box titled "Level 3 and 4," on your copy of the Sample Chore Chart.

The maximum weekly allowance will vary depending on your age child. Some parents of teenagers pay $10.00 to $20.00 per week and truly expect them to budget and use their own money for personal expenses

In the example, I was comfortable with a maximum allowance of around $10.00 per week for a 13-year-old child. I calculated it this way: $10.00 divided by 7 days = $1.42 (rounded off to $1.50 per day). I then wrote this amount ($1.50) in the correct box directly below Level 3 and 4-see shaded area below:

Chore Chart

Level 1 and 2	Level 3 and 4	Month of:
	1.50	1 2 3 4 5 6 7 8 9 10 11 12 13 14 15 16 17 18 19 20 21 22 23 24 25 26 27 28 29 30 31

Next, you need to determine how much allowance will be paid if your child does less than a perfect job. If you have chosen a perfect or fail approach, you would pay full pay or nothing ($1.50 per day for perfect and nothing per day for fail). Since I feel children need room to grow into doing perfect jobs, I would suggest at least three levels of pay. $1.50 per day for a perfect job, $.75 per day for an adequate job or nothing for a poor job. In the example, I chose to have six levels of pay for work done and therefore divided the $1.50 per day maximum into six parts. Perfect = $1.50 for the day. Near Perfect = $1.10 for the day. Above average = $.80 for the day. Average = $.50 for the day. Below average = $.30 for the day and Poor = $.20 for the day.

I then placed these amounts in the Level 3 and 4 column under the $1.50 maximum. See shaded area below:

Chore Chart

Level	Level	Month of:																
I and 2	3 and 4	1	2	3	4	5	6	7	8	9	10	11	12	13	14	15	16	17
	1.50																	
	1.10																	
	0.80																	
	0.50																	
	0.30																	
	0.20																	
Daily Total Due:																		

To figure out how much daily allowance your child will receive if he is on Level One or Two, you simply reduce the amount you have decided upon for Levels Three and Four. If you have decided upon a pass/fail approach, you would take the daily allowance for Levels Three and Four and reduce it. Divide it in half ($1.50 divided by 2=$.75 per perfect day on Level One and Two). In the example, I have six levels of pay. I decided to reduce the daily allowance by half for Perfect and Near Perfect jobs. For less than perfect jobs, I decided to reduce the daily allowance by more than half. For Level One and Two I decided to pay:

Perfect = $.75 for the day. Near Perfect = $.55 for the day. Above Average = $.30 for the day. Average = $.15 for the day. Below Average = $.05 for the day and Poor = $.00 for the day. In this way, I am offering children additional incentives to get and stay on Levels Three and Four.

I then wrote the amounts outlined above in the correct boxes directly below Level 1 and 2-see shaded area:

Chore Chart

Level 1 and 2	Level 3 and 4	Month of: 1	2	3	4	5	6	7	8	9	10	11
0.75	1.50											
0.55	1.10											
0.30	0.80											
0.15	0.50											
0.05	0.30											
0.00	0.20											
Daily Total Due:												

Chores will be checked by:

Level # 1 and 2:   weekdays _____   weekends _____   *Level #3 and 4:*   v

Clothing allowance: date due _____   earned _____   not earned _____

If you have chosen to use a graduated allowance which is tied to the quality of job done (as I have outlined on the last five pages), you will not have to decide how many points to assign chores. The pay levels dictate how many points chores are worth. In the example, I chose to have six pay levels, therefore, I will have six point levels which tie into the pay levels. 5 points for perfect, 4 points for near perfect, 3 points for above average, 2 points for average, 1 point for below average and 0 points for poor. We need to write the points under each calendar day on the line indicated-see shaded area on the next figure.

Finally, to finish the comprehensive chore chart, add in monetary bonuses and consequences. As you can see by the finished Comprehensive Chore Chart Sample in Chapter Nine, page 138, I chose to add a $.15 per day bonus for not wasting and deduct for wasted food, water, electricity or toll calls (900 numbers). Examine your priorities and add to or deduct from your children's allowance(s) according to your needs or level of patience.

Chore Chart

Level	Level	Month of:								
I and 2	**3 and 4**	I	2	3	4	5	6	7	8	9
0.75	1.50	5	5	5	5	5	5	5	5	5
0.55	1.10	4	4	4	4	4	4	4	4	4
0.30	0.80	3	3	3	3	3	3	3	3	3
0.15	0.50	2	2	2	2	2	2	2	2	2
0.05	0.30	I	I	I	I	I	I	I	I	I
0.00	0.20	0	0	0	0	0	0	0	0	0
Daily Total Due:										

Chores will be checked by:

Level # I and 2:   weekdays _____   weekends _____   *Level #3 and 4:*

Clothing allowance: date due _____   earned _____   not earned ___

Simple Chore Chart

If you have decided not to tie allowance into the chores, you can still combine chores and behavior by using the Simple Chore Chart. To do this, decide how many points chores will count for in your "Daily Total" points. The points need to be chosen on the basis of your grading-perfect to failure. Some people are comfortable with the simple perfect or failure and would choose the number one-one point for perfect and zero points for failure. While others would prefer for there to be more grading room. In the sample, I have six grades. 5=perfect, 4=very good, 3=average, 2=below average, 1-poor and 0=failure. Once you have chosen how many "grading points" you wish to offer your child, mark the maximum point value (5 in the sample) on the top line under each day. Refer to your copy of the Simple Chore Chart in Chapter Nine, page 137. Breaking maximum to minimum, (In the sample, 4, 3, 2, 1, 0) write each successively lower point value across each line (under each day, 1 to 31).

Begin by writing in your high or perfect point values under each day of the month on the top line. When you have finished, your chart should look something like:

Simple Chore Chart

Month:	1	2	3	4	5	6	7	8	9	10	11	12	13	14	15	16	17	18	19	20	21	22	23	24	25	26	27	28	29	31
	5	5	5	5	5	5	5	5	5	5	5	5	5	5	5	5	5	5												
	4	4	4	4	4	4	4	4	4	4	4	4	4	4	4	4	4	4												
	3	3	3	3	3	3	3	3	3	3	3	3	3	3	3	3	3	3												
	2	2	2	2	2	2	2	2	2	2	2	2	2	2	2	2	2	2												
	1	1	1	1	1	1	1	1	1	1	1	1	1	1	1	1	1	1												
	0	0	0	0	0	0	0	0	0	0	0	0	0	0	0	0	0	0												

Chores will be checked by:

Level # 1 and 2:   weekdays _____   weekends _____   Level #3 and 4:   weekdays: _____   weekends_____

Clothing allowance: date due _____   earned _____   not earned _____

As with the Comprehensive Chore Chart, you may want to opt for bonuses (not wasting) and consequences for waste. These will work equally well if they are points which add directly into your Daily Total or money which does not affect the Daily Total. Either way, add the lines necessary, i.e. "Plus" for bonuses and/or "Less Waste" for waste. Then write in the points or money under each day of the month, across each line as I have done in the samples. See Chapter Nine Chore Chart samples.

Totaling Chores

For normal purposes, you will not go beyond Level 3 as Level 4 is for emancipating children. See the chapter titled, "The Separating Adolescent." Thus, unless you wish to have more levels in your system or if you have an adolescent, you will probably be wise to keep your system to four levels: 0=no privileges, 1=minimum privileges, 2=greater privileges and 3=greatest amount of privileges.

Totaling chores is done in much the same way as totaling behavior. See Chapter Three, pages 58-59.

After you have set up either the Comprehensive Chore Chart or the Simple Chore Chart, you are ready to track your child's accomplishments regarding chores. Please be aware that if you have room on your behavior chart, you can simplify things even more by including chores and/or bonuses/consequences for conservation/waste directly on your Behavior Chart.

To keep track of your child's progress on a daily basis, simply mark (with one of the colored markers) how well the chores were completed. This is done by highlighting how many points he earned in the same way that you mark his behavior on the Behavior Chart. If your child did all the chores, and did them well, mark the "5". This would mean that, if he is on Level 2, in the sample, he would earn 75 cents and if he is on level 3, $1.50, or twice what Level 2 kids receive. If only a half-hearted attempt was made, you might mark 2 points on the Chore Chart and he would earn 50 cents for the day at Level 3. It would be 15 cents for the day on Level 1 or 2. If you have decided not to include allowance on your Chore Chart, this marking procedure is the same.

Marking chores for a half-hearted attempt on January 11 would look like this if you include allowance on your chore chart.

Chore Chart

Level	Level	Month of: January										
I and 2	3 and 4	I	2	3	4	5	6	7	8	9	10	11
0.75	1.50	5	5	5	5	5	5	5	5	5	5	5
0.55	1.10	4	4	4	4	4	4	4	4	4	4	4
0.30	0.80	3	3	3	3	3	3	3	3	3	3	3
0.15	0.50	2	2	2	2	2	2	2	2	2	2	2
0.05	0.30	I	I	I	I	I	I	I	I	I	I	I
0.00	0.20	0	0	0	0	0	0	0	0	0	0	0

Daily Total Due:

Chores will be checked by:

Level # I and 2:   weekdays _____   weekends _____   *Level #3 and 4:*   wee

Clothing allowance: date due _____   earned _____   not earned ____

(Mark at the intersection of the shaded areas with a colored marker.)

Marking chores for a half-hearted attempt on January 11 would look like this if you DO NOT include allowance on your chore chart:
(Mark at the intersection of the shaded areas with a colored marker.)

Simple Chore Chart

Month: January	1	2	3	4	5	6	7	8	9	10	11	12	13	14	15	16	17	18	19	20	21
	5	5	5	5	5	5	5	5	5	5	5	5	5	5	5	5	5	5			
	4	4	4	4	4	4	4	4	4	4	4	4	4	4	4	4	4	4			
	3	3	3	3	3	3	3	3	3	3	3	3	3	3	3	3	3	3			
	2	2	2	2	2	2	2	2	2	2	2	2	2	2	2	2	2	2			
	1	1	1	1	1	1	1	1	1	1	1	1	1	1	1	1	1	1			
	0	0	0	0	0	0	0	0	0	0	0	0	0	0	0	0	0	0			

Chores will be checked by:

Level # 1 and 2: weekdays _____   weekends _____   Level #3 and 4:   weekdays: _____ weekends_____

Clothing allowance: date due _____   earned _____   not earned ____

Again, it will be up to you to determine how much allowance your child may earn. Decide the highest figure you are comfortable with depending on the child's age, responsibility, and financial needs (does he buy all his school supplies and clothes or just pay for an occasional movie?). Then set up the Chore Chart in such a way that only by doing all of his chores perfectly will he be paid the full amount agreed upon. Anything less will earn him a decreasing amount of allowance.

The allowance given in the sample may seem rather high, on observation. However, the children in the sample earn all of their spending money. When a child has to save and budget their own money, allowance means more. When money is tied to chores, they become more motivated to do chores. Decide what rate of pay is appropriate for your age child. Remember, maximum points and allowance are for doing ALL the chores on the list for that day.

Checking Chores

At the bottom of the Chore Charts, you will notice a time when chores will be checked depending on the level of the child. I suggest that you adhere to your time table and not check before or after the scheduled time. It has been my experience that a child can drive you crazy checking each chore, re-doing the chore, and re-checking. In my house, the following rules apply:

1. Chores will be checked at the time stated.

2. If the child finishes a chore ahead of time, he must "keep it clean" until checking time.

3. The child has one chance to re-do a sloppy job, but loses a point. (See "Work Doesn't Need Re-Doing" on the Behavior Chart.)

4. If a child decides not to do his chores, he will be sent to his room until he decides to do chores. (See "Resistance to Structure").

If he eventually decides to do his chores to rejoin the family, he would still get an Automatic Negative Day if he didn't have his chores done on time but would not forfeit his allowance because he did do his chores.

Saving Money

You will notice that, on the Sample Comprehensive Chore Chart (Chapter Nine, Page 138), I encourage the children to develop good habits. This is accomplished by giving the children the chance to earn bonus money for not wasting food, electricity, water, or abusing the telephone. How many of us suffer the 1-900-Blues? The way this waste abuse was curtailed was by entering a section for "Saving Money." The child receives a 15 cent per day bonus if he does not waste during the day. Below the "saving money" heading I wrote in all the ways the children were being negligent. Please note that the chart was set up so that the parent could easily mark, in green, each time water or electricity was wasted by highlighting the charge (35 cents per offense) each time a light was left on or water left running (25 cents). Space was left to mark the cost of a food item wasted (left out of the refrigerator, or a sandwich being prepared and left to die on the sofa). Next, because I did experience the "toll charges" by the local telephone company, I opted to charge both children 35 cents per day until all "1-900" calls were stopped. Thus, I didn't need to conduct a "whodunit;" I simply charged them both.

Not Me!

Anyone who has more than one child has experienced the "I didn't do it!" syndrome. I set up a rule for charging the children which was very effective in stopping the "Not me!" response. When the parents ask, "Who left the light on in the kitchen?" and one of the children confessed, that child was charged. If neither child confessed, both were charged. This ended the battle of "whodunit." Very soon they both decided to be responsible regarding waste since they would rather avoid charges and get all the money they earned. The money you save here will probably pay for a trip to Tahiti for the whole family.

Totaling Chore Points

When totaling the Chore Chart, you must first create a line on your Behavior Chart on which you will write in the Chore Points Earned each day. This will not be necessary if you combine the chores and behaviors on the same chart. I suggest that you place the Chore Points Earned line below your Behavior lines and above Bonuses and/or Automatic Negative day line(s)-if any. A good position for the Chore Points Earned line would be the shaded line in the example.

Behavior Chart

Month:	1	2	3	4	5	6	7	8	9	10	11	12	13	14	15	16	17
Homework:	5	5	5	5	5	5	5	5	5	5	5	5	5	5	5	5	5
Behavior:																	
Following the Rules	1	1	1	1	1	1	1	1	1	1	1	1	1	1	1	1	1
Work Doesn't Need Redoing	1	1	1	1	1	1	1	1	1	1	1	1	1	1	1	1	1
Clean Up After Myself	1	1	1	1	1	1	1	1	1	1	1	1	1	1	1	1	1
Chore Points Earned																	
Bonuses:																	
Helping Points	1	1	1	1	1	1	1	1	1	1	1	1	1	1	1	1	1
Listening Points	1	1	1	1	1	1	1	1	1	1	1	1	1	1	1	1	1
Automatic Negative Day:																	
Disrespect																	
Breaking Grounding																	
Lying																	
Didn't Heed Warning																	
Not Going to Time Out																	
Not Doing Chores At All																	
Daily Total Due:																	

11	Points = Perfect Day
9	Points = Pass Day
7	Points = Negative Day

Negative Days Brought Forward 2
Negative Days Wiped Out (date) 4/18/00

Report Card Average		Hours to Study
B		1/2
C		1
D		2
F		3

After you have marked the "grade" for the chores done during the day, (a score of 5 to 0 in the example), write the score for the day on the Chore Points Earned line of the Behavior Chart. If you are not tying allowances to chores, you have finished with the Chore Chart for the day unless you have bonuses for saving or deductions for waste.

If your child had done a mediocre job on chores January 11, you would mark the 2 directly under the day "11" on your chore Chart and write this number on the Behavior Chart under day "11" on the Chore Points Earned Line. (See shaded area)

Simple Chore Chart

Month: January		1	2	3	4	5	6	7	8	9	10	11	12
		5	5	5	5	5	5	5	5	5	5	5	5
		4	4	4	4	4	4	4	4	4	4	4	4
		3	3	3	3	3	3	3	3	3	3	3	3
		2	2	2	2	2	2	2	2	2	2	2	2

Chores will be checked by:

Level # 1 and 2:   weekdays _____   weekends _____   *Level #3 and 4:*   weekd

Clothing allowance: date due _____   earned _____   not earned _____

Behavior Chart

Month: January	1	2	3	4	5	6	7	8	9	10	11	12	13	14	15	16	17	18	19	20	21
Homework:	5	5	5	5	5	5	5	5	5	5	5	5	5	5	5	5	5	5	5	5	5
Behavior:																					
Following the Rules	I	I	I	I	I	I	I	I	I	I	I	I	I	I	I	I	I	I	I	I	I
Work Doesn't Need Redoing	I	I	I	I	I	I	I	I	I	I	I	I	I	I	I	I	I	I	I	I	I
Clean Up After Myself	I	I	I	I	I	I	I	I	I	I	I	I	I	I	I	I	I	I	I	I	I
Chore Points Earned	5	3	4	5	1	0	3	5	3	4	2										
Bonuses:																					
Helping Points	I	I	I	I	I	I	I	I	I	I	I	I	I	I	I	I	I	I	I	I	I
Listening Points	I	I	I	I	I	I	I	I	I	I	I	I	I	I	I	I	I	I	I	I	I
Automatic Negative Day:																					
Disrespect																					
Breaking Grounding																					
Lying																					
Didn't Heed Warning																					
Not Going to Time Out																					
Not Doing Chores At All																					
Daily Total Due:																					

	Report Card Average	Hours to Study	When to
11 Points = Perfect Day			
9 Points = Pass Day	B	.5	7:30 p.m. to
7 Points = Negative Day	C	1	5:00 p.m. to
	D	2	4:00 p.m. to
Negative Days Brought Forward 2	F	3	3:00 p.m. to
Negative Days Wiped Out 4/18/00			

Totaling the Behavior Chart when you have included points for chores is the same as totaling the Behavior Chart without chores. (See page 59.) You will need to add the total possible chore points into your equation for a "P day" (perfect day), a "+ day" (plus day) or a "- day" (negative day). Thus, adding chores to our example on page 59, there are 11 possible behavior points + 5 possible chore points = 16 possible points per day.

If you refer back to pages 55 and 56, chores have already been added into the example and have been spread between "P", "+", and "-" days. Therefore, on January 11, Johnny's Behavior Chart would look like the example on page 89, if he receives 2 points for chores (marked on the Chore Chart and written on the Chore Points Earned line of the Behavior Chart). I highlight in green if the child fails to do adequately in a behavior area and highlight in pink if the child earns bonus points. Thus, on January 11, the Behavior Chart is marked with a green mark for homework (homework was not done), no additional green marks (Johnny did not lose any additional behavior points). Johnny did earn bonus points for helping and listening so I marked both of the bonus point areas in pink. Finally, Johnny received no automatic negative day marks (no green marks below "Automatic Negative Day)." See example on page 89.

To total the day, you would begin with a possible 11 behavior points and deduct all green marks.

- I I possible behavior points
- -5 points (a green mark for homework). Add to this any pink bonus points;
- +2 bonus points (marked in pink-helping and listening). Add to this chore points;
- +2 chore points (marked on Chore Chart and written on Chore Points Line)
- =I0 points for the day.

On the lower left hand corner of the Behavior Chart, you have written in the point spread for "P", "+" and "-" days. Look and see what kind of day 10 points equals. The example says Johnny had a "- day" and I would write 10 in the Daily Total Due and mark it with green marker (pink marker = perfect, yellow marker = + and green marker = - days).

Behavior Chart

Month: January	1	2	3	4	5	6	7	8	9	10	11	12	13	14	15	16	17	18	19	20	21	22
Homework:	5	5	5	5	5	5	5	5	5	5	5	5	5	5	5	5	5	5	5	5	5	5
Behavior:																						
Good Attitude	1	1	1	1	1	1	1	1	1	1	1	1	1	1	1	1	1	1	1	1	1	
Household Peace	1	1	1	1	1	1	1	1	1	1	1	1	1	1	1	1	1	1	1	1	1	
Doing What I'm Asked	1	1	1	1	1	1	1	1	1	1	1	1	1	1	1	1	1	1	1	1	1	
Following the Rules	1	1	1	1	1	1	1	1	1	1	1	1	1	1	1	1	1	1	1	1	1	
Work Doesn't Need Redoing	1	1	1	1	1	1	1	1	1	1	1	1	1	1	1	1	1	1	1	1	1	
Clean Up After Myself	1	1	1	1	1	1	1	1	1	1	1	1	1	1	1	1	1	1	1	1	1	
Chore Points Earned:	5	3	4	5	1	0	3	5	3	4	2											
Bonuses:	Mark in green for deductions above this line. Mark in pink for bonuses below this																					
Helping Points	1	1	1	1	1	1	1	1	1	1	1	1	1	1	1	1	1	1	1	1	1	
Listening Points	1	1	1	1	1	1	1	1	1	1	1	1	1	1	1	1	1	1	1	1	1	
Automatic Negative Day:	Mark in green below this line for Automatic Negative Days.																					
Disrespect																						
Breaking Grounding																						
Lying																						
Didn't Heed Warning																						
Not Going to Time Out																						
Not Doing Chores At All																						
Daily Total Due:	16	AN	15	AN	AN	11	14	15	13	14	10											

	Report Card Average	Hours to Study	When to Stu
16	Points = Perfect Day		
14	Points = Pass Day		
12	Points = Negative Day		

Report Card Average	Hours to Study	When to Stu
B	.5	
C	1	
D	2	
F	3	

Negative Days Brought Forward 2
Negative Days Wiped Out 4/18/00

In the example above, I used the letters "AN" to signify an Automatic Negative Day for breaking a Bottom Line Rule. I did not write in the Daily Total Due because the child earned a negative day regardless of the number of points he earned. Additionally, using the formula of seven negative days in a three month period = dropping down a Level, Johnny has just dropped a Level as of January 11.

2 Negative Days brought forward (See lower left hand corner of example.)

+1 Negative Day-Automatic for not going to time out on January 2.

+1 Negative Day-Automatic for lying on January 4.

+1 Negative Day-Automatic for not heeding warning on January 5.

+1 Negative Day-Below 13 points for the day on January 6.

+1 Negative Day-Below 13 points for the day on January 11.

=7 Negative days total, with the wipe out day of February 5.

Johnny will have to get seven perfect days in a row in order to get back up to the Level he was on.

Remember, if you decide to use points rather than money as rewards for not wasting and consequences for wasting, these points must be added into the total for "P," "+" and "-" days.

If you do not tie allowance to chores, you have finished tracking for the day. If you do tie allowance to chores, you must do one additional step. Write in the allowance for the day at the bottom of the chore sheet on the line titled Daily Total Due and in the proper day column.

Add up and write in the "Total Allowance Due".

1. After you have marked the "point value" for the chores, look directly to the left and find the allowance due for the day under the column marked Level 1 and 2 or Level 3 (depending on what level your child is on).
2. Add the "saving money" bonus, if earned.
3. Subtract any amount for waste, marked in green as you caught it during the day.
4. Write this total due in the Total Due box at the bottom of the Chore Chart.

If you do not use monetary amounts for "Saving and Waste" you can skip numbers two and three above.

As an example, let's assume Johnny is on Level 3 and on January 11, he did a "2 point" job on his chores, left a light on, left water running, was charged 35 cents for (900) toll calls and left the bread out (50 cents). He:

Earned	.50	for chores
		(amount due under Level 3 for a "2 point" job)
Lost	.35	for leaving a light on
Lost	.25	for leaving the water running
Lost	.35	for toll phone calls
Lost	.50	for leaving the bread out on the counter
Total	-.95	

You would mark a MINUS .95 in the Total Due box at the bottom of the sheet under the day of the month. Since Johnny ended up owing us money for the day, this amount would be deducted from his allowance at the end of the week.

Even though Johnny went down from Level 3 to Level 2 on January 11, he still receives the allowance for Level 3 for January 11 because he didn't drop a level until the end of the day. On January 12, he would earn the allowance due for level 2 or 15 cents if did a "2 point" job again on January 12.

Chore Chart

Level 1 and 2	Level 3 and 4	1	2	3	4	5	6	7	8	9	10	11	12	13	14	15	16	17	18	19	20	21	22	23	24	25	26	27	28	29	31
												Month of: January																			
0.75	1.50	5	5	5	5	5	5	5	5	5	5	5	5	5	5	5	5	5	5												
0.55	1.10	4	4	4	4	4	4	4	4	4	4	4	4	4	4	4	4	4	14												
0.30	0.80	3	3	3	3	3	3	3	3	3	3	3	3	3	3	3	3	3	3												
0.15	0.50	2	2	2	2	2	2	2	2	2	2	2	2	2	2	2	2	2	2												
0.05	0.30	1	1	1	1	1	1	1	1	1	1	1	1	1	1	1	1	1	1												
0.00	0.20	0	0	0	0	0	0	0	0	0	0	0	0	0	0	0	0	0	0												
+ PLUS +																															
.15 each day there is no waste		.15	.15	.15	.15	.15	.15	.15	.15	.15	.15	.15	.15	.15	.15	.15	.15	.15	.15	.15	.15	.15	.15	.15	.15	.15	.15	.15	.15	.15	.15
- LESS WASTE -																															
food = cost of item												.50																			
water .25 per time water is left on												.25																			
electricity .35 per time light left on												.35																			
telephone abuse = cost of call												.35																			
Daily Allowance:												.95																			

Chores will be checked by:

Level # 1 and 2:   weekdays _____   weekends _____   Level #3 and 4:   weekdays: _____   weekends_____

Clothing allowance: date due _____   earned _____   not earned _____

The example Chore Chart below reflects what Johnny's Chore Chart should look like on January 11.

Thus, the Chore Chart tells you and your child the amount of money due him for the day. I pay allowance on Saturday after chores are completed. I have included a second, simplified chore chart sample in Chapter Nine to help you see the options. The possibilities are endless. Let your family's needs and your imagination guide you.

Clothing Allowance

You will notice that there is a "Clothing Allowance" area at the bottom of the Chore Chart. This was set up because it finally became too much to shop for clothes with the children. I did not want to spend the outrageous sums on "junk" clothes desired by my adolescents. To circumvent power struggles, I decided to allow each child a specified sum every other week with which to buy their own clothes (not including shoes and coats). The children were responsible for washing and putting away all of their clothes before they would get their clothing allowance. Since this system was installed, the children are learning how to shop and budget their money. They are asking for advice on where to shop and which additions are the most practical to their wardrobe. They are also taking much better care of the clothes they have.

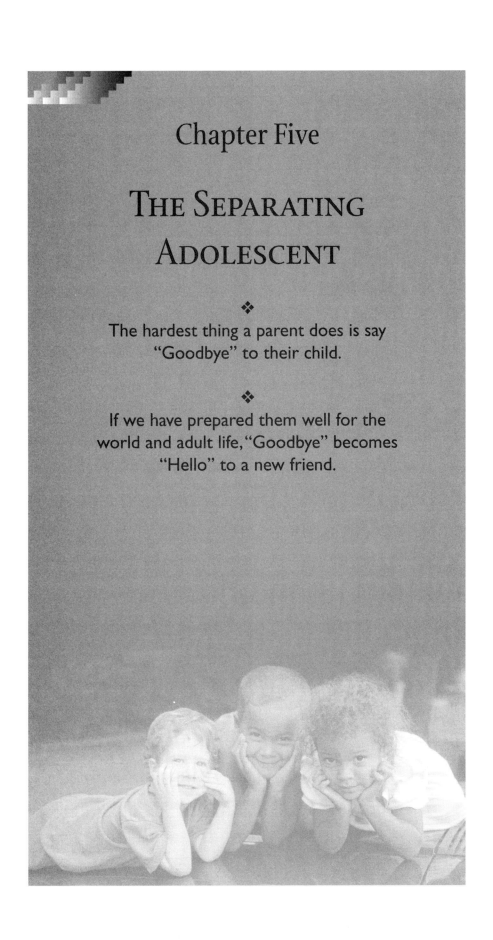

Chapter Five

THE SEPARATING
ADOLESCENT

❖

The hardest thing a parent does is say
"Goodbye" to their child.

❖

If we have prepared them well for the
world and adult life, "Goodbye" becomes
"Hello" to a new friend.

The Separating Adolescent

The following article was written by a young man while a Senior at Pueblo Central High School. It is printed here with his kind permission.

This article is not something those of faint heart or queasy stomach would enjoy. In fact, it is not something anyone would enjoy reading. It is graphic and tragic.

I have included "Wouldn't it be a Drag?" in this book for the purpose of communicating to young adults who still maintain the illusion of invincibility. You, as parents, will decide whether to share this article with your child. I will simply say I would rather upset the sensibilities of my step-children than to have tragedy strike. While there is no guarantee that this article or any other communication will convince a young adult that cars and drinking are something which require care and maturity, I insisted that my daughter read this before she "got her set of keys".

Wouldn't it be a Drag?

by Bryant Frazer, Pueblo Central High School

"Wouldn't it be a drag to lose your driver's license?" You've seen the posters. They show a typical teenager and his typical girlfriend looking typically depressed because of having to sit on the ground in a parking place at a drive-in movie. The bottom of the poster admonishes: "Don't drink and drive." Does that image terrify you? Does it strike horror into your heart? I'll bet that's one of your mortal fears, isn't it? Having to walk to a drive-in movie? Give me a break.

I'd like to throttle the condescending Madison Avenue twit who came up with that little jingle. He's so far removed from reality that he actually believes the stereotypical teenager exists. You know, the one that has no more pressing concern than how he's going to get to the next movie marathon at the local drive-in. He actually thinks that his cutesy campaign addresses the problem. He can't even come close. Drunk drivers have nothing to do with drive-in movies, driver's licenses, or anything else that's in the experience of most teenagers. Drunk drivers have a lot to do with mortal danger. They have a lot to do with stupidity. They have a lot to do with death.

Are you one of them? You drive cross-town to a party in the country where you're going to go and get wasted, unworried about how completely screwed over your head might be when you start the car to get back home? It's natural. You never feel like you can't drive, especially if you're "just" buzzed. As far as your little drunken mind is concerned, you couldn't be in better shape to hit the highway and blaze into Pueblo at top speed. You even did it once and you came out okay. Pretty proud of yourself, aren't you?

Yeah, really proud until you roll that Mustang of yours across the median as you blaze into town at top speed. Then you'll have another chance to be proud of yourself if you can think a coherent thought or roll yourself three feet in your wheelchair once you come out of that coma. IF you get out of it. It's one BIG hangover.

But maybe that doesn't bother you so much. It's your life—why shouldn't you be able to ruin it whichever way you want to? The problem with that kind of idiotic reasoning is that most of the time, the drunken moron behind the wheel isn't the only victim of an accident. Think about this one, Mr. Macho Man, the next time you drive your girlfriend home from a kegger. You're driving on I-25 windows down, stereo blasting Sammy Hagar—and sure enough, you're too stupid to drive 55. You're somewhere up around 100. You feel a spinning sensation as your brain goes wonky for a second, see a huge shadow come down on the right side of your car as you drift into the other lane, and the world blacks out.

You wake up on the pavement, bruised up and bloody, but feeling no pain. That keg in your stomach isn't making anything fuzzy and exciting anymore—it just makes you puke on the asphalt. You see that you've coughed up a little blood, but still don't feel anything. You turn your head, and once your vision clears, you see your girlfriend. All you can see is a torn, twisted body bulging in a grotesque lump under a filthy pink sweater. Her face has already been torn to shreds by the glass of your windshield, and the cops are still trying to scrape what's left of her out from between the bucket seat and the dashboard. The engagement ring you gave her is already lost, probably smashed into the road by one of the countless cars driving by slowly, faces pressed to windows, staring and pointing at what used to be your lover.

You close your eyes, try to shake the whole thing off like a bad dream but it's not a hallucination, it's not a drive-in movie, and you know it's not a poster in the counselor's office. You stare at the road, see a car that swerved out of the way of your wreck with its front end embedded in the side of another on the other side of the road. On the ground far below the highway, something very large, probably a tanker truck, is burning, and you hear sirens that scream at you from all directions. A voice behind you makes it clear to someone else that more people have already been pronounced dead, and somehow you know it's just the beginning.

After you recover from that one great party, you slowly come to the cold realization that eight people's deaths will hang in your dreams forever. All because you had to prove how well you could hold on to your liquor. All the blood, because you had to be a Highway Hero. *Wouldn't that be a drag?*

Level 4 is for those of us who are helping our adolescents through the issues of separation. It is for those children who are entering the last year of high school or going to college while living at home. Because this is a distinct period of growth with different rules and reactions, I will discuss some ways that Levelling can be modified to meet the needs of our older children.

Through experience, I have found that it is necessary to dramatically alter Levelling while maintaining the concept and flavor for our "young adults." This is a time when we need to add the finishing touches in helping them prepare to function as adults in an adult world. This means that our expectations and responses must shift. We need to stop expecting them to participate fully in the life of the family and point them towards the discovery of self-sufficiency. Very soon, they will need to do everything on their own. We can help them in this transition by asking them to do as much as possible by themselves—using us only as counsel. It will be much easier for them to learn, while they have us to fall back on, than it will be to learn the hard way from the world.

For Emancipating Adolescents, I Suggest:

- Instead of utilizing the chart, rely more heavily on the rules.
- Prepare a "consequences" sheet which states what the consequences are for breaking the rules.
- Have all parties sign the bottom of the sheets noting that they understand and agree.
- Again, the options are up to you and your environ ment. Do not be afraid to add new rules and conse quences as unanticipated situations arise.

Charging for Broken Rules

Adolescents often have a part-time job, and I have found that charging for broken rules can be very effective i.e. $5.00 per half hour late for curfew or $2.50 for forgetting to wash the dishes. Forgetting to wash the dishes? Yes, I believe that a person should contribute to his environment unless he is paying for his rent, utilities, food, etc.

If your adolescent works outside the home, try to refrain from helping him avoid mistakes. The best lesson about being late for work is the chewing out from the boss or even getting fired! Remember, soon he will not have you to fall back on, and the mark of a successful parent is the one whose child is able to function well in the world without parental help.

Adolescents and The Car

A note regarding driving either your car or their own: I feel the adolescent should be responsible for his own insurance. Cars statistically last at least 3 years longer when an adolescent contributes to the cost of the car. I strongly suggest that the car does not move without the child paying for auto insurance 3 months in advance.

When it came near the time when my daughter would get her license, I told her that she would have to be on Level 4 in order to learn and have the privilege of driving. My Level 4 criteria was: 1. That she remain on Level 3 for six months prior to getting her driver's license. 2. That she maintain a "B" average in school. Additionally, should she fall from Level 4 to Level 3, or achieve below a "B" average in school, she would lose her driver's license for the six months it took her to get back to Level 4 and/or get and maintain a "B" average.

Adolescent Rebellion

Last, and most unfortunate, rebellion strikes even at this level. If you are having a problem with the feeling that, "No matter what I do, he just won't follow the rules," I suggest a "put up or shut up" approach. Often, the adolescent will feel he's all grown up and should be his own boss. When this occurs, remind him that you are still supporting him. If he wishes to be his own boss, he may do so either by paying for his room and board, (make the amount the same as he would pay outside of your home) or moving out, if they are of legal or emancipated age.

If he chooses either of these alternatives, and handles the responsibilities involved, he has proven to you and the world that he is, indeed, ready to be his own "boss." If, however, he wants you to continue to support him, then he must follow the "rules of the house."

Sample Level 4 Structure

I would like to offer, as an example, what one family used for their separating adolescent. Feel free to use this structure, or adapt it for your use. This family decided that there were just three choices they would offer to their child. They spelled out these choices along with the benefits and consequences:

Option A - Family

You can be a full member of the family with all the rights, privileges and responsibilities of a family member.

Rights and privileges
- Live in our family home
- Have your food provided
- Have much of your clothing provided
- Have responsible use of family property such as TV, phone, living areas, etc.
- Receive a $20 per week allowance
- Have available such personal needs as clothes washer, etc.
- Have personal care items such as soap, toothpaste, etc., provided
- Have the privilege of owning and driving your own car
- Live in an atmosphere of growing mutual trust and respect
- Have support with questions, problems and concerns

Responsibilities
- Be a contributing member of the family, working to help establish trust and respect
- Show a cheerful and responsible attitude in dealing with all the members of the family
- Adhere to agreed upon hours
- Home within one hour of quitting time at work
- Home at agreed upon time at other times
- Notify us where you are and when you'll be home
- Attend all classes on time
- Pick up your room and bathroom every day

- Clean your room and bathroom once each week (vacuum, dust, clean fixtures)
- Be responsible in your use of family property and living areas:
  - Pick up after yourself in all areas (family room, garage, basement, etc.)
  - Be responsible in your use of items such as phone, TV, food, etc., keeping use to reasonable amounts and time
- Ask permission before using the property of other family members
- Do not work on the car at home (in driveway)
- Do your share of the family chores
- Make your car payments to us on the first day of each month
- Assume other responsibilities as necessary for the good of the family
- Consequences for not living up to the responsibilities of a member of the family:
  - $10 fee for each missed school class or for not adhering to agreed upon hours
  - Loss of allowance for abuse of other responsibilities
  - Loss of car privileges or other specific privileges for abuse of responsibilities
  - Potential loss of the family option for suspension from school or serious abuse of trust

Option B - Tenant

You can purchase room and board from us with limited rights, privileges and responsibilities.

Rights and privileges
- Room and bathroom at $225 per month
- Limited food at $50 per month
- Utilities at $25 per month
- Freedom to come and go as you please, including class attendance, work and social hours, etc.

Responsibilities
- Room and board payments are made promptly on agreed upon date
- Install and assume financial responsibility for your own phone
- Pick up room and bathroom daily
- Clean room and bathroom once a week
- Ask permission for us of household property and living areas
- No use of other's property without explicit agreement
- No working on car on the property
- Ask permission before eating any food
- No personal items left in household living areas
- Provide for your own personal needs (clothes washed at a Laundromat, etc.)
- Purchase your own personal care items
- Other responsibilities as necessary to maintain a positive landlord/tenant relationship.

Option C - Living on Your Own

While this option is the ultimate goal, you must decide under what circumstances it occurs. You can choose to emancipate naturally while still maintaining a relationship as a member of this family with the rights, privileges and responsibilities of a family member. Or you can chose (or force us to choose for you), severing your relationship with the family and losing those rights, privileges and responsibilities.

The Family

Snow flies on a cloudy day and my mood is light.

Rainbows sparkle and mash my windows and for me, all

is right. First we rolled, then we flew down the crusty,

virgin, run. Crystal tapping our faces, chill stinging our

throats and lungs, as we sloughed back up the hill to

repeat the screams of ever faster, ever farther, downhill

ploughs.

Hey God, we're here, there's joy and love

in our hearts and in this day you gave us. We have the

peace in spirit called a family and we thank you!

Mom

Chapter Six

LEVELLING WITH CHILDREN UNDER 7

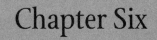

Because our children start out so dependent
It's hard for us to know when and how to
let them go so they can grow.

Levelling With Children Under 7

Children as young as 2 and 3 have benefited from the structure and sense of accomplishment Levelling offers. Changes have to be made to simplify the system so a young child can understand the Levelling concept and keep interested in his progress. Parents of very young children have used a tape recorder rather than paper and pen to set up Levelling for their children.

Bottom Line Rules and Automatic Negative Day behavior should be used. Children need to know the limits in order to achieve proper behavior. Try to limit these rules to a few important ones, and keep them simple and straightforward.

Instead of increasing independence (an 8:30 weekend curfew for a 5-year-old is obviously inappropriate), I have found that increasing rewards depending on how the day and week are going work better.

This is an example of what one family is doing with their 5 year old:

Chores
Pick up bedroom
Set table for dinner
Brush teeth
Take a bath
Make bed
Pick up family room before bed time
Clear dinner table
Behavior
Obeying first time asked
Not fighting with sister
Good attitude
Getting dressed quietly in morning
Eating neatly
Not interrupting when parents are on the phone
Automatic Negative Day
Bad attitude
Tantrum
Talking back
Not behaving at the grocery store

Depending on the age of your child, you may need to simplify the system even more. Following is an example of a very simple chart for a small child. Keep the number of behavior/chores short, and "grade" the day for how it is going overall by using smiley, straight, or frown faces. For a really great day, a sticker works wonders.

As your child's maturity level increases, you will want to increase responsibilities and freedoms. You can do this by adapting or converting your very simple chart to a simplified point system. As an example for the older child, I gave each chore/behavior one point, and there were a total of 13 possible. Since I found that using the perfect "+" and "-" day classifications to be too complicated, I made it simple: If he gets 11 points out of 13, the day is considered "good". I've noticed that placing the chart in a prominent place at the child's eye level (perhaps the refrigerator) reinforces his accomplishments or reminds him when he needs to do better.

It was too hard for the child to get 7 good days in a row so I started with 3 good days, and worked up to getting 4 good days in a row to earn a big reward. Set up rewards depending on the child's ability to achieve. We don't want to discourage him by demanding more than he is capable of achieving. Gradually, as he becomes able to fulfill our expectations and his responsibilities, increase the difficulty of achievement.

If he has a good day, he can pick one of the rewards previously agreed upon and written down for the daily good behavior. For example: watching a favorite TV program, spending special time with us, playing with Play Dough, candy, after dinner "special me" time, or trading in colored stickers for money. It makes children so proud to be able to spend their own nickel or dime at the store.

If he had a bad day, he may not have any of the rewards. In addition, one of his daily, favorite things that is standard practice around the house (playing with a friend, a favorite toy, dessert, bedtime story, etc.), is forbidden for the day.

A young child's chart might look something like this:

A Typical Child's Chart	Mon	Tue	Wed	Thu	Fri	Sat	Sun
Morning	☹	☹	☺	☺	☺		
Afternoon	😐	☺	☺	☺	☺		
School	😐	☺	☺	☺	☺		

If he has 4 good days in a row, he gets a bigger reward: a kite, an inexpensive toy, a book, a visit to Dairy Queen for ice cream, or a trip to the zoo, etc.

For a young child, try not to determine the number of good days needed to earn a big reward strictly for that reward. To them, a 99 cent kite can be as important as a trip to the zoo. Be realistic with yourself and your time. In Chapter Nine, you will find award cartoons to use for positive reinforcement. Feel free to reproduce them and use them as you wish. Pin them on your child's shirt or hang them on his door. Have him color and display them on a special bulletin board, etc.

You could work out your level system so that if your child has a certain number of negative days in a given period of time, something is taken away for an extended time. For example, 2 negative days in a 2 week period, and his bike is taken away for a week. Once again, because of the age of the child, it is very important to keep the time periods short and the rules as simple as possible. Feel free to add to or modify the list of behaviors and chores as you go along. It is amazing how much a young child can comprehend and accomplish if we give him a chance.

It is just as important to have consequences which won't punish the parent as it is to have rewards. Consequences teach our children that when we do what's expected, we get "paid" and if we don't, we get "punished." It is much easier for a child to learn this lesson about the way the world "works" while having the security of our care. It is a shock for some kids to leave home and then find out that they can't tell the world how they want things to be.

The Saga of SuperMom

We're lying around the pool - Las Vegas or somewhere - beautiful people in the sun...

I look up with a sense of dread - Oh, my God! The lawn furniture is devouring its inhabitants!

I look down and mine is starting to move...

I sit up with a start knowing something is wrong, shaking the dream from my head. I look at the clock - 7:30 - the kids have been playing with it again! Oh, my God! The board meeting is at 8:00 - I'm supposed to present...

Run to the shower. No time for coffee - No hot water! - A cold shower will wake me up...I guess - But this cold? Who used all the hot water? Is the pilot out?

Get dressed, pink suit, white blouse - Must look my best - stockings, damn! a run, New pair? -None left - Wonder if they'll notice this run?

To the car, I look O.K., I really do, Start car, start!

Finally, O.K., I'll be about 20 minutes late - if I'm lucky they won't notice...Hey-you, Lady! You're going 20 and the speed limit is 45, Move it! Please?...I'll pass. as soon as the 10 cars behind me pass us both...1...2...3...9!

After this one, Oh, my God! A red light, Let's see 12 more to pass me first. O.K. put on lipstick and drum my fingers on the dash...I'd forgotten this light is so long...How many now, 15 cars! Deep breath, Relax, Relax, Relax, Relax!

Into the parking lot 8:30, If I'm lucky...Run! I love you desk - Papers for the meeting right where I left them...They'll call me in 15 minutes? - Great! Get coffee and compose myself, What a morning!...Coffee room - Great fresh coffee - Finally...Back to my desk, Around this corner and Oh, my God! "No, Jim, I'm fine, It only burned a little bit and for a minute, Are you O.K.? Did any splash on you? No, it's just getting a little cold now as it trickles all down my front like this."...No time to get home before, They're ready for me now? What'll I say about the coffee?...

I'm glad that's over, mortified, that's what I was - Oh well, it's behind me now..."Mr. Jones, May I go home and change?" "Yes I really need to, I know there's a deadline, but I'm all soggy and clammy and thanks, I'll hurry"...

Unlock the car, Deep breath, O.K. That's it! The worst is past, Let's see, Work late, O.K., Groceries on the way home tonight, O.K., Glass of wine and a hot tub! I deserve it, boy what a morning!...Forgot to lock the front door, Oh, my God! I forgot to put puppy out! Boy did she need to go! O.K. brat, to the back yard with you...Now, what'll I wear? Oh, my God!, Not my new gray pumps, The ones I couldn't really afford!, I thought puppies liked slippers best, I see got those too! Well, maybe the shoe repair can fix the pumps, I just wish you'd left the heel on that one...

"Yes, Mr. Jones, it'll be done today, I'll work till 7:00 and have it on your desk for tomorrow morning"...What?, Oh, my God!, the School Principal on which line? "Yes, Mr. Chee, is Peter..., Thank God!", "I see"..." and how did he get them up to the ceiling?"..."Twang?, With a fork?"..."Yes, I see"..."Mrs. Grey's head?" "Well, what goes up"..."No!", "I don't think he learned this trick at home, We eat"..."Yes, Sir!"

Home sweet home, I didn't think I'd make it. Unload the groceries, wine, tub. What a day, I just can't believe it!...Well, a letter from mom, someone loves me, great timing mom, how could you know..."After thinking over your last telephone call"...God, mom, I wish you wouldn't write I'm doing the best I..."Hi, Guys, You wouldn't believe"..."What? a hole in the fence? She bit Jacy Lauson? Isn't Jacy's dad an attorney?..."The pound? First thing in the morning? What's the number again?...

One question, God and only one...**Does anyone else have days like this?**

Mom

Chapter Seven

COMMUNICATING WITH
YOUR CHILDREN

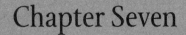

All human relations are based on communication.

❖

Without the ability to let others clearly
understand us *we are truly alone*.

*A*ll these
things shall love do unto you
that you may know the secrets of your
heart, and in that knowledge become
a fragment of Life's Heart.

Kahlil Gibran

Once Levelling has eliminated the negative interaction in your
home, you will want to establish new communication techniques.
These new skills will replace the yelling, arguing and badgering which
used to take up all of your time. I suggest you use the following techniques as the need arises. Monthly family meetings can be useful.
Meetings can help clear the air, refine your system and keep in touch
with how everyone feels about how it's going. It is very important to
listen to every member's objections and input. Alter, as necessary, the
way things are done.

Affective Clarification Technique (ACT)

I developed ACT for use in therapy. It is very useful while making the transition to the Levelling system. It can be used between you and any person who cares about maintaining a good relationship with you. It can be done by the whole family or just two people. It gives a chance to vent hostilities in a safe, non-threatening manner. ACT will help clean out all of the negatives which accumulate in your relationships. In this way, room is made for a refocus on positives and love. If there are major issues between the two parents that need to be resolved, it would be best to do that first, in private, before involving the children. When using ACT as a family, you will find it to be most effective when focusing on family issues. You can always use ACT for "spot prevention" when hostilities arise with a "parent and child" or "child to child".

Just because you are part of a family and love each other, does not necessarily mean that you like each other's behavior all of the time. Being part of a family and living in the same house does not mean you will all share identical views. These differences cause conflict, and are perfectly normal in all families. ACT helps to resolve these conflicts.

Start ACT by holding hands in a circle. Older kids may want to do this without holding hands. All listeners must look at the eyes of the person talking and may not interrupt. To start, each person takes a turn saying to each person around the circle: "I'm mad / I feel sad / or I feel hurt, etc.) when...". An example might be, "I'm mad when you yell at me in front of my friends," or "I'm mad when you pick up the phone while I'm talking on it." Some people feel uncomfortable saying "I'm mad," and this can be changed to "I don't like" or whatever you feel comfortable with. I strongly recommend using the word "mad" because more often than not, the emotion honestly is mad and, in most cases, not mere dislike.

It's okay to stop and discuss/problem-solve what has just been said as long as you continue with the exercise to the end. Sometimes, when things get overly emotional, it may be helpful to "time out" (break the exercise for 10 minutes to cool off). It's very important to return and finish the exercise, even if you need to time out several times before the end.

Continue with each person taking his turn unloading all of the negatives until everyone says "I have no more mad (or negative feelings)." Sometimes it will happen that one person will have a lot of hurt or anger left after the others have expressed all of theirs. It is important to allow everyone to get rid of all of their negative feelings. Just let the person keep expressing until his anger is "empty." Often, you will find that some of the anger is illogical or ridiculous. Don't judge yourself or others about whether or not the anger or love is "rational." Our feelings need expression whether verbal or by action. ACT allows us to express verbally rather than by "acting out". Feelings are, more often than not, irrational, but they poison our relationships just the same.

It is important that we start by loving ourselves; this is the root of self-respect from which ego strength, values, and love of others grows.

The final step in ACT is "loving." This is a critical step and should never be skipped. It re-sets our perspective and allows us to focus on the positive qualities of ourselves and our family members. You may be surprised at just how powerful "family love" is!

After all the people have expressed their negative feelings, we want to re-focus ourselves on the positive. To do this, we follow the same rules we used to get rid of the negative, except we focus on the positive by saying one thing I (love / like / respect) myself because... Then, while looking at the person's eyes and state one thing I love about each person in the group (I love you because...). Again, "like" can be substituted for "love," but is not as effective. It is important that we start by loving ourselves; this is the root of self-respect from which ego strength, values, and love of others grows.

I suggest that you go around the circle at least two times. For example, Dad might say, "I love myself because I'm a good provider", and then going around to each person in the group say, "I love you, Jane (or whomever you are addressing) because you're such a good cook." Then Mom goes around, starting with herself first and speaking to each person in the group. Then each child takes a turn. When you

have gone around the entire group one time, repeat the exercise. I suggest going around the circle a minimum of two times. You may go around as many times as you like so each person has at least two turns to express their love.

ACT has been very beneficial in cleaning out negative feelings, promoting understanding, identifying problems, resolving them, and helping people to love/appreciate each other. While it may be difficult at first to express your anger, after a time it will be a welcomed relief. If the relationship(s), are under an inordinate amount of stress, you may want to repeat the process once a week tapering to once a month to maintain great relationships.

Agreeing to Disagree

Communication is based on trust. If we are to communicate honestly, we must trust that we will not be judged for what we say. The worst error we can commit—the one which will dissolve all honest communication—is to tell someone that they are wrong, bad, stupid, etc. These are value judgments. We all, even our children, have the right to our beliefs without judgment. To help our children learn and grow, we need to help them learn to question their views. People who live in the same family won't always agree. It is greatly preferable to "agree to disagree" than to judge another for their views.

The worst error we can commit—the one which will dissolve all honest communication—is to tell someone that they are wrong, bad, stupid, etc.

Agreeing to disagree might be used when a child makes a decision which is not tremendously harmful. One of the primary areas where a parent may agree to disagree is clothing. As an example, Peter, my adolescent, was a "Skater." This is a group in school who live, breathe, and eat skate-boarding. They have developed a unique dress code to accompany their interest. Basically, I agreed to disagree on the way Peter chose to dress. Peter wanted to buy pants which were very baggy and wear them with T-shirts which had "Skater" logos. I told Pete: "I think you look much better in slacks and a sport shirt, but I understand that your clothes help you to identify with your group at school." I did not judge Peter. I told him calmly that his choice of clothing is not my "thing." I agreed to disagree. I would like to point out that this extends only to where I believe that something will not be harmful to Pete. When Peter asked if he could pierce his ear and wear an earring, I told him he could not. I stated that: "A hole in your ear lobe is something you may regret as an adult. If, when you move out and are on your own, you still want to wear an earring, then it will be your decision. It is my job as a parent to help you see the consequences of your actions. I feel piercing your ear would have consequences you would regret for a long time. Because of this, you may not pierce your ear."

Reflective Listening

Reflective listening is a way to help someone clarify what they are saying and ensure that communication is taking place. "Are you hearing what I'm saying?" "Yes, I am. You said…" To do this, we must be non-judgmental and prepared to agree to disagree. It is important that we establish eye contact, be open and not distracted by other things. The dialogue is opened by one person saying what is on his mind:

Speaker: "I hate all my teachers!" The listener states what he heard the speaker say.

Listener: "You hate all your teachers." If the speaker agrees that the statement is correct, the listener can ask questions to help clarify.

Listener: "Why do you hate all your teachers?"

Speaker: "Because they're all dumb."

Listener: "Because they're all dumb?"
Speaker: "Yes!"

Listener: "Why do you think they're all dumb?"

Speaker: "Because my math teacher gave me an "F" on my test because he thought I was looking at Sally's paper."

Now you have gotten to the real problem, and can work with your child to resolve it. Again, be non-judgmental, and help your child resolve his problem. Don't do it for him. Ask him questions about how he feels. Ask what he can do to resolve the misunderstanding, cope with his feelings, or avoid the same problem in the future.

Reflective listening can be used during ACT to work through highly emotional problems when they arise. It's best, if both people are upset, to have both people reflective listen (repeat back what the speaker just said) before responding. You will be surprised how many disagreements are simply a misunderstanding of what was said.

We can teach our children to be better listeners from early on. Reflective listening is a powerful tool to use with children with ADD. This skill will carry over to their ability to listen in school. Before they repeat back to you what you just said, have them learn to repeat it within their self first. For younger children, have their brain tell their heart what you just said. This technique helps all children process better and "get it". Once they've done this they will be able to focus and reflective listen with you much better.

Reflective listening is a wonderful technique to use in all relationships. With teens, it bridges the "generation gap". This is because we all want "to be heard" on a human level. Once we all get past our own agendas and truly listen to one another, the walls drop and the communication deepens to a more connected, human place. This is where we ALL have common ground. Tensions ease and a child, no matter what age, feels loved.

"I" Messages

I messages are a great way to avoid being judgmental. They also establish who "owns" the problem. *I messages* are a way of stating how what's happening is affecting the speaker. Instead of judging the person and escalating the problem, you have told your child (or anyone your are in conflict with) how you feel (something they can empathize with) when they do something. *I messages* contain three parts: first, the speaker's feelings (I feel), second, the behavior or situation (when you), and third, the reason (because). When you identify the reason or the "because," you have identified the problem, which can be worked out to, hopefully, everyone's satisfaction. You are ready to problem-solve! An *I message* should be framed in three parts, with words like: When you... I feel... because... With practice, *I messages* become easy to form. They will greatly reduce the friction in the situation since they identify which part of the problem belongs to which person. If you are finding the problem difficult to resolve because feelings are deeply hurt, or everyone is clinging to their position, don't forget to include a time out (a chance to cool down) and reflective listening (be sure you both are talking about the same thing) with your *I messages*. An example of an *I message* is, "I feel angry when you talk back to me in front of your friends because it's embarrassing!" not a *You Message*: "You spoiled, ungrateful brat, how dare you talk back to me in front of people!"

From the *I message* you can resolve the issue:

"Would you like it if I put you down in front of my friends?"

   "No."

"How would it make you feel?"

   "Pretty bad."

"Then what can we do about it?"

   "I didn't think about how it would sound before I said it. I'll try to think before I talk."

"Okay, that might work, but I want to let you know in advance that if it happens again, I will time you out in front of your friends. I didn't today, because I didn't want to embarrass you. I'm going to write it down in the House Rules right now, so you won't forget what the consequences are for talking back. Do you understand?"

   "Yes, Mom, I'm sorry."

"I'm sorry we had this problem too, Hon."

A Dialogue for Healthy Coping Skills

I have spoken of Coping Skills and their importance in our children's emotional health. What follows is a verbal approach which is helpful in helping our children learn Healthy Coping Skills. There are 10 components to the Healthy Coping Skills dialogue. They are designed to teach children good coping skills. This dialogue can be done with a child of any age providing they are old enough to carry on a conversation. I shall list the components and show you how they fit into an actual occurrence between a mother and her daughter, Suzie.

Components

- Be non-emotional-this is your child's problem, not yours.
- Do NOT run interference-your child has earned the consequences from his behavior and will not learn that he has control over his life unless you allow him to deal with those consequences.
- Ask your child how he feels about the situation.
- Ask your child the how, why, and what of the situation.
- Ask your child what the consequences of his actions are.
- Ask your child if the prices were worth the payoffs (there are usually more than one of each).
- Ask your child what (if anything) he's going to do different next time (this helps him learn to project probable consequences for future behavior).
- Empathize and help your child know that we all have the same feelings and similar dilemmas.
- Suggest alternatives, which others have used, which he may not be familiar with.
- Let the child know that you make mistakes and learn from them.

This is a dialogue Suzie had with her mother. It is an example of the interaction which is designed to help a child learn healthy coping skills. Suzie had planned to cut her last class at school in order to talk with a boyfriend. Her boyfriend said that he would never talk to her again if she didn't talk to him during that period (which he had free). She had Tom, her younger brother, call the school and pretend to be Suzie's father who excused her from that class. The school became suspicious because Tom did not sound like an adult and called Suzie's mother to find out if the father had called.

Component #2
When Suzie's mother found out what Suzie had tried, she asked the school to administer the maximum consequences for the offense-even though this was the first and

only time Suzie had broken any school rules. The consequence for Suzie was a one day suspension. Suzie's mother went to pick Suzie up from school. On the drive home, Suzie and her mother discussed what had occurred:

Component #3
Mother: "How do you feel about what just happened?"
Suzie: "Embarrassed and mad."

Component #4
Mother: "Why did you have Tom call the school to excuse you?"
Suzie: "Because Jim said he'd never talk to me again if I didn't talk to him at last class today. I was afraid he meant it and wouldn't like me anymore."

Component #5
Mother: "You have broken a serious rule and your home consequences are that you are now demoted from Level three to Level zero. So, what are the consequences for trying to cut last hour today?"
Suzie: "I got suspended and am on Level zero."
Mother: "What does being on Level zero mean in this situation?"

Suzie: "That I'm grounded from the phone and life until I'm on Level one, probably a week."
Mother: "So, now you aren't going to be there to talk with Jim, and you can't call him and tell him why, right?"
Suzie: "Yes."

Component #6
Mother: "Those are pretty heavy consequences, was it worth it to try to cut last hour?"
Suzie: "No."

Component #7
Mother: "What are you going to do next time something like this happens?"

Suzie: "I'll tell Jim that I'll call him after school and if that isn't good enough, he can just not talk to me ever again."

Component #8
Mother: "That's a good response. I know that sometimes it isn't easy to say something like that to a person when they put you in the position Jim did. I think you learned something very important from this. I'm sorry that it had to cost you so much, but I'm very proud of you for being able to come up with such a good solution if something like this happens again. You're becoming quite an adult. That isn't easy-I know, I remember how hard it was when I was your age."

Component #9
Mother: "The only thing you're lacking right now is that adults try to project what the consequences will be and if the consequences are worth the payoffs BEFORE they do something. That way, they are sometimes able to avoid paying the high prices you just paid."

Component #10
Mother: "You know, I was in a similar situation. Want to hear about it?"

Conclusion

These communication techniques are useful in many situations, not just those involving your children. Try them with your spouse, parents, and other relatives. Try saying, "what I heard you say was, (re-state the statement)-is that what you meant?" Use "I messages" with anyone. To help you decide which technique is appropriate, remember this: whoever is having the emotional reaction is the "owner" of the problem. If it is you, use "I messages," if it belongs to someone else, use reflective listening. These communication techniques will help you avoid problems and misunderstandings, and open doors to better communication.

Chapter Eight

HAPPY LEVELLING

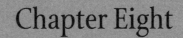

My intent in writing this book is twofold:

*To keep parents and children from having
to endure unnecessary pain.*

*To show parents how to raise healthy,
happy children.*

Brian

Happy Levelling

As you can see, with Levelling, you are limited only by your imagination and needs. Levelling gives you time to enjoy your children and create a positive environment rather than constantly arguing. Your children know where they stand every minute of the day. They know the "when, how, where, and what" of their responsibilities and privileges without your having to beg, plead, remind and follow up. You no longer have to play "Mommy can I?" "Why can't I, Dad?" and "Everyone else does." All you have to do is refer to the system and say, "Level Two kids go to the movies one time per week. I'd sure like for you to be able to see that movie too! Sure hope by next week you will be on Level Two so you can go!"

Connecting

I talk with many people who are feeling like "bad parents" because, as their children grow older they are spending less and less time with them. Depending on the age of your child, you may or may not have this feeling. A newborn needs you constantly, not only to provide for their physical needs, but also for emotional support and loving feedback. As your children mature, they will be providing more and more of their physical and emotional needs for themselves. Instead of feeling that somehow we have alienated our children or made them not want to be around us, we should be pleased that we are doing such a good job of parenting. It is a blessing that our children feel secure enough to venture out on their own!

As children grow, sometimes starting as young as two, what they need is to "touch base" with you. This is what the "terrible two's" are all about. Your child is beginning to separate a little and test his ability to stand alone and fend for himself. He, understandably, becomes unsure of himself and frequently comes running back for reassurance. By the time he is four or five, however, you will find that he is checking in for quick hugs. He will bounce ideas and behaviors off you to test them out. After that, he's' back to exploring the world.

If you wish to test this, go to your child with the intention of giving him as much of your time and attention as he wants. Depending on his age and what is going on in his life at the moment, it could be any-where from 30 seconds to 30 minutes. Certainly, there will be times (a trip to the zoo, a family vacation, a quiet Sunday afternoon) when you will spend large amounts of time with your children. On a day to day basis, what they want are frequent, brief opportunities to check in to see that you're still "there" for them. This is, of course, when they're not preoccupied with friends or activities. Children in day care or school are interacting with teachers and peers all day and will probably only want 15-20 minutes of your undivided attention when they get home. Certainly, the more time you have to spend with your children the more you can enhance your relationship. However, in the busy world we live in, focus more on quality time with your children. In this way, they will have the security of your bond and guidance, no matter how busy it gets.

One of the biggest "guilts" parents experience is the feeling that somehow we're cheating our children because "we're not home all day like our mothers were." I see parents trying to compensate for this by being "friends" with their children. Our children need the security of our being parents, not friends. They HAVE friends. If we don't parent them, then they have too many friends and no parents! Later, when they are adults, there will be a great opportunity to be friends with your children.

When we were children, yes, mom was home but she didn't spend the days with us. If she had, we would have hated it. We, like our children were busy experiencing the world and growing. We were out playing in the neighborhood or at school and "checked in" for meals or at curfew. Yes, a great many of our children have lost the extended families we had. This is having a great effect on the generation we are rearing. However, this means that our children need the security of our parenting even more. Our children do not need more things. Our children need the security of a PARENT who's emotionally present and a loving structure which they can depend upon for safety and guidance.

Having Fun With Your Children

And now that you have more time to have fun with your children, here are some suggestions for play.

You may want to divide the following into three categories of activities that take three different range of times (i.e. 30 minutes, 1-2 hours and one-half / full day). Given the amount of time you have , you can let your child know what category will work for you that day.

Participation Sports:

Volleyball
Fishing
Camping
Hiking
Biking
Swimming
Softball
Sailing
Croquet
Golfing
Catch
Ice skating
Rollerblading
Sledding
Snowball fights
Jogging
Football
Canoeing
Rafting
Water skiing
Basketball
Hockey

Non-sport Activities:

Picnics
Cards
TV & TV sports
Telling stories
Reading aloud
Board games
Talking
Cooking
Shopping
Visiting people
Dancing
Wrestling on the floor
Pillow fights
Water fights
Building snowmen
Building tree forts
Eating out
Going for a drive
Praying/reading scripture
Singing
Concerts
Plays
Movies
Zoo
Circus

Museum
Planetarium
20 questions
Charades
Sewing
Crafts
Amusement parks
Electric trains
Crossword puzzles
Evening walks
Vacations
Telling jokes
Family project
(garage sales,
building models etc.)

Chapter Nine

EXAMPLES *and*
WORKSHEETS

Examples and Worksheets

This chapter contains examples and copy masters of the various worksheets and charts. Make copies of all copy masters (except "Notes Sheets") before writing on them.

If you wish to contact the Institute for Integration Therapy our Levelling hot line address and telephone number is:

I. F.I.T.
P.O. Box 620430
Littleton, Colorado 80162
E-Mail: DrBrody@AscendCoaching.com
(303) 979-0319

 Example

Levels and House Rules

Bottom Line Rules
- Disrespect
- Breaking grounding
- Lying
- Not going to time out
- Didn't heed warning
- Chores not done at all = an evening in room, no games or books until ready to do chores

Level 0
- Grounded from phone and outside
- No privileges except eating
- No TV

Level 1
- Can't leave house until chores are done
- Can't go anywhere without verbal permission
- Must leave phone number where you will be
- Must leave exact time when you will be back
- Weekday curfew 6:00
- Weekend curfew 8:00
- May not spend night at friend's house
- May have friends overnight 1 time per week
- No friends in until chores and homework done

Level 2
- May attend after school activities as long as chores done on time
- Can't go anywhere without verbal permission
- Must leave phone number where you will be
- Can be 15 minutes late if you call
- Weekday curfew 7:00
- Weekend curfew 9:00
- May spend the night at friend's house 1 time per week
- May have friends overnight 1 time per week
- Friends may wait while chores being done

Level 3
- After school freedom as long as chores and homework done on time
- May leave note where you can be reached by
- phone and time coming home
- Can be 1/2 hour late if you call
- Weekday curfew 8:00
- Weekend curfew 10:00
- May spend night at friend's house or have friend overnight 2 times per week
- May ride bicycle
- May have friends in for chores and study hall
- A license to drive with a certain grade point average

129

Copy Master

Levels and House Rules

Bottom Line Rules: (Breaking bottom line rules is an automatic negative day.)

_____

_____

_____

_____

_____

Level 0

_____

_____

_____

_____

Level 1

_____

_____

_____

_____

Level 2

_____

_____

_____

_____

Level 3

_____

_____

_____

_____

 Example

Daily Chores

Tuesday / Thursday / Saturday / Monday – Sweep front walk

1. *Make bed and clean room:*
   Bed must have two sheets and a pillowcase at all times. The sheets must be washed weekly. All clothes must be hung up, nothing on the floors and room vacuumed, if needed.

2. *Dishes on Sunday / Monday / Wednesday / Friday:*
   Dishwasher must be run and emptied, if needed. All appliances washed down: front and sides of refrigerator, stove and dishwasher, stove knobs and clock washed, microwave inside and out, all counter appliances and under everything on counter must be washed. Clean sink with cleanser, put silverware and pots and pans where they belong, wash pots and pans and all large items and wooden handled knives by hand, rinse and leave in drainer to dry. Empty drainer—if you do not, you will dry and put away everything daily. Straighten rugs on kitchen floor.

3. *Upstairs bath:*
   Wipe down toilet, drainboard, sink, mirror, pick up any stuff on floor, sweep floor on Saturday, mop and wash on 2nd Saturday of month.

4. *Vacuum the stairs.*

5. *Trash checked daily:*
   Take to garage on Sunday night; clean kitchen container on Sunday.

6. *Wipe and clear kitchen table.*

 Example

Motivation List

Likes	Dislikes
Cookies	Staying home Friday night (you needn't ground for a week to make an impression!)
Skateboard	
Bike	Extra work/chores
Movies	Being ignored
Rides	Being sent to room with no TV, stereo etc.
Baby-sitting	Having friends call and being grounded from the phone.
Telephone	
Hair Dryer	Missing out on "family time."
Makeup	Having mom and dad refuse all privileges until I get my behavior under control. Whatever the request is, the answer is No!
Curling Iron	
Use of car - Mom & Dad's	
Use of car - Mine	Not having All things on the "like list."
Stereo	Writing contracts about what I can do differently in the future. Having mom and dad show me the contracts when I don't do differently.
Tape Deck	
VCR	Sitting quietly in the room with mom (or my room) and thinking about what I did, why it was wrong, how it has made the people involved feel, why I wouldn't like someone doing it to me and what I'll do differently next time, then telling mom and/or dad all this before I can go play.
TV	
Playing Video Games	
Going to the Mall	

Copy Master

Motivation List

Likes	Dislikes

 Copy Master

Monthly Budget and Life Plan

Name: _____

I plan to get a job doing: _____

This job pays $ _____ per month.

I must have the following experience to get this job.

_____

_____

_____

_____

_____

This education will cost $ _____ and will be paid for in the following manner:

	$
	$
	$
	$

This form and the monthly budget on the next page, are very useful for adolescents who think that school and grades are unimportant and that they are ready to be on their own. Parents should point the aspiring adult in the right direction to get the information needed, but then let them gather the information and fill in the blanks by themselves. In this way the child learns the reality the parent already knows rather than the parent appearing to be *lecturing* the child.

 Copy Master

Monthly Budget

Income Tax: .... $ _____ Per Month

Rent/Mortgage; .... $ _____ Per Month

Clothing: .... $ _____ Per Month

Food: .... $ _____ Per Month

Telephone: .... $ _____ Per Month

Entertainment: .... $ _____ Per Month

Health Insurance: .... $ _____ Per Month

Car Insurance: .... $ _____ Per Month

Water/Sewer: .... $ _____ Per Month

Travel/Vacation .... $ _____ Per Month

Gifts: .... $ _____ Per Month

Public Service .... $ _____ Per Month

Loans for: **Loans amount:**

Car (year: _____ make: _____) $ _____ $ _____ Per month

TV/Furniture: $ _____ $ _____ Per month

Dishes/Linen/Pots and Pans $ _____ $ _____ Per month

Total Monthly Expenses: $ _____ **Per month**

Totals:

Total Monthly Income: $ _____ Per month

Less: $ _____ Per month

Total Monthly Expenses: $ _____ Per month

= Over/<Short> Monthly:

 Example

Simple Chore Chart

Month:	1	2	3	4	5	6	7	8	9	10	11	12	13	14	15	16	17	18	19	20	21	22	23	24	25	26	27	28	29	31
Daily Chores																														
Make Bed																														
Clean Bedroom																														
Take Out Trash																														
Clear Dinner Table																														
One Day Per Week																														
Clean Bathroom - Monday																														
Wash Sheets - Saturday																														
Take Trash to Curb - Sunday																														
Sun/Mon/Wed/Fri:																														
Wash Dishes																														

Chores will be checked by:

Level # 1 and 2:   weekdays _____   weekends _____   *Level #3 and 4:*   weekdays: _____   weekends_____

Clothing allowance: date due _____   earned _____   not earned _____

Copy Master

Simple Chore Chart

Month	1	2	3	4	5	6	7	8	9	10	11	12	13	14	15	16	17	18	19	20	21	22	23	24	25	26	27	28	29	31

Chores will be checked by:

Level # 1 and 2:   weekdays _____   weekends _____   Level #3 and 4:   weekdays: _____   weekends _____

Clothing allowance: date due _____   earned _____   not earned _____

 Example

Comprehensive Chore Chart

Level 1 and 2	Level 3 and 4	1	2	3	4	5	6	7	8	9	10	11	12	13	14	15	16	17	18	19	20	21	22	23	24	25	26	27	28	29	30	31
																Month of:															
0.75	1.50	5	5	5	5	5	5	5	5	5	5	5	5	5	5	5	5	5	5	5	5	5	5	5	5	5	5	5	5	5	5	5
0.55	1.10	4	4	4	4	4	4	4	4	4	4	4	4	4	4	4	4	4	4	4	4	4	4	4	4	4	4	4	4	4	4	4
0.30	0.80	3	3	3	3	3	3	3	3	3	3	3	3	3	3	3	3	3	3	3	3	3	3	3	3	3	3	3	3	3	3	3
0.15	0.50	2	2	2	2	2	2	2	2	2	2	2	2	2	2	2	2	2	2	2	2	2	2	2	2	2	2	2	2	2	2	2
0.05	0.30	1	1	1	1	1	1	1	1	1	1	1	1	1	1	1	1	1	1	1	1	1	1	1	1	1	1	1	1	1	1	1
0.00	0.20	0	0	0	0	0	0	0	0	0	0	0	0	0	0	0	0	0	0	0	0	0	0	0	0	0	0	0	0	0	0	0
	+ PLUS +																															
.15 each day there is no waste		.15	.15	.15	.15	.15	.15	.15	.15	.15	.15	.15	.15	.15	.15	.15	.15	.15	.15	.15	.15	.15	.15	.15	.15	.15	.15	.15	.15	.15	.15	.15
	- LESS WASTE -																															
food = cost of item																																
water .25 per time water is left on		.25	.25	.25	.25	.25	.25	.25	.25	.25	.25	.25	.25	.25	.25	.25	.25	.25	.25	.25	.25	.25	.25	.25	.25	.25	.25	.25	.25	.25	.25	.25
electricity .35 per time light left on		.35	.35	.35	.35	.35	.35	.35	.35	.35	.35	.35	.35	.35	.35	.35	.35	.35	.35	.35	.35	.35	.35	.35	.35	.35	.35	.35	.35	.35	.35	.35
telephone abuse = cost of call																																
Daily Allowance:																																

Chores will be checked by:

Level # 1 and 2:   weekdays _____   weekends _____   *Level #3 and 4:*   weekdays: _____   weekends_____

Clothing allowance: date due _____   earned _____   not earned _____

Copy Master

Comprehensive Chore Chart

Level and	Level and	Month of:																												
		1	2	3	4	5	6	7	8	9	10	11	12	13	14	15	16	17	18	19	20	21	22	23	24	25	26	27	28	29	31
Daily Total Due:																																

Chores will be checked by:

Level # 1 and 2:   weekdays _____   weekends _____   Level #3 and 4:   weekdays: _____   weekends _____

Clothing allowance: date due _____   earned _____   not earned _____

 Example

Behavior Chart

Month:	1	2	3	4	5	6	7	8	9	10	11	12	13	14	15	16	17	18	19	20	21	22	23	24	25	26	27	28	29	31
Homework:	5	5	5	5	5	5	5	5	5	5	5	5	5	5	5	5	5	5	5	5	5	5	5	5	5	5	5	5	5	5
Behavior:																														
Following the Rules	1	1	1	1	1	1	1	1	1	1	1	1	1	1	1	1	1	1	1	1	1	1	1	1	1	1	1	1	1	1
Work Doesn't Need Redoing	1	1	1	1	1	1	1	1	1	1	1	1	1	1	1	1	1	1	1	1	1	1	1	1	1	1	1	1	1	1
Clean Up After Myself	1	1	1	1	1	1	1	1	1	1	1	1	1	1	1	1	1	1	1	1	1	1	1	1	1	1	1	1	1	1
Chore Points Earned																														
Bonuses:																														
Helping Points	1	1	1	1	1	1	1	1	1	1	1	1	1	1	1	1	1	1	1	1	1	1	1	1	1	1	1	1	1	1
Listening Points	1	1	1	1	1	1	1	1	1	1	1	1	1	1	1	1	1	1	1	1	1	1	1	1	1	1	1	1	1	1
Automatic Negative Day:																														
Disrespect																														
Breaking Grounding																														
Lying																														
Didn't Heed Warning																														
Not Going to Time Out																														
Not Doing Chores At All																														
Daily Total Due:																														

11	Points = Perfect Day
9	Points = Pass Day
7	Points = Negative Day

Negative Days Brought Forward	2
Negative Days Wiped Out (date)	4/18/00

Report Card Average	Hours to Study	When to Study
B	1/2	7:30 p.m. to 8:00 p.m.
C	1	5:00 p.m. to 6:00 p.m.
D	2	4:00 p.m. to 6:00 p.m.
F	3	3:00 p.m. to 6:00 p.m.

Copy Master

Behavior Chart

Month:

	1	2	3	4	5	6	7	8	9	10	11	12	13	14	15	16	17	18	19	20	21	22	23	24	25	26	27	28	29	31

___ Points = Perfect Day

___ Points = Pass Day

___ Points = Negative Day

Negative Days Brought Forward |___|

Negative Days Wiped Out (date) |___|

Report Card Average	Hours to Study	When to Study

Notes

Notes

Notes

Notes

HIP HIP HOORAY!

You
did a great job!

APPROVAL
The Seal of

Awarded To:

Super Star

Awarded To:

_____

For:

_____

Appendix

Services

Speakers

ASCEND Professional Speakers Bureau offers you the best of seasoned, experienced, professional speakers who give talks and workshops on a variety of topics.

Lists & Addresses

If you are interested in a more complete list of ASCEND speakers, topics, or video presentation of talks, please contact our offices at:

Institute for Integration Therapy
P.O. Box 620430
Littleton, Colorado 80162

1-888-458-8543 (toll free)
1-888-4-LUV-KID
1-(303)-979-0319

www.AscendCoaching.com

DrBrody@AscendCoaching.com

Tapes

Accessing Relaxation Tape
(This is available for parents and children.)

Parent Coaching is also available by phone.

Presentations

Talks presented by Brian Brody, Psy.D. include:

For Adults
- Lessons From Littleton
- Suicide/Violence Prevention
- *Levelling*, A Guide to Positive Parenting
- City Gangs/Suburban *Kiddie Cults*
- *Teaching the Heart* - for teachers
- *Integration Therapy* and **how it works**
- Two Hours to Positive Discipline
- Avoiding Burnout
- How to Balance Work With Family
- Building Successful Family Relationships
- Step-Parenting
- Single Parenting
- Stress Reduction
- Drug Prevention
- Helping Yourself / Help Others
- Behavior Management in the Classroom
- Many More

For Children / Adolescents
- Helping Yourself / Help a Friend
- Winning
- Overcoming Destructive Behaviors
- Saying No To Drugs

About The Author

Brian Brody, Psy.D. is a noted psychologist, author, consultant, speaker and parent coach who appeared on CBS EVENING NEWS, NBC NEWS, PHIL DONAHUE and INSIDE EDITION television shows.

Brian has presented numerous talks, classes and workshops on a variety of issues, privately, and in conjunction with public schools, agencies and colleges.

Brian is a consultant for the State of Colorado PTA, and was a board member for Family Tree. Brian is the current Director of the Institute for Integration Therapy.

In response to the difficulties he personally overcame while blending a step-family, Brian has developed a mix of traditional therapeutic methods and common sense which has successfully helped thousands of families and individuals.

A graduate of University of Denver, Washington University and the University of Colorado, Brian's community involvement has included: serving on the Governor's Commission on Suicide Prevention, co-founder for Suicide Prevention Allied Regional Effort - State of Colorado (SPARE). Consultation for the Department of Social Services and participation on KIMN'S "Kids - Dying for Attention and KWGN's "For Kids Sake."

For more information, call: (303) 979-0319 or write:

Institute for Integration Therapy
P.O.Box 620430, Littleton, CO. 80162

www.AscendCoaching.com

DrBrody@AscendCoaching.com